3 Days in Washington Γ Guide

Welcome to Washington, D.C., the capital of the United States and a city full of history, culture, and excitement. With its impressive monuments, museums, and government buildings, there is no shortage of things to see and do in this bustling metropolis. Whether you're a first-time visitor or a frequent traveler to D.C., this guide is designed to help you plan your trip and make the most of your time in the city. From iconic landmarks to off-the-beaten-path attractions, we'll take you on a journey through the best that Washington, D.C. has to offer.

So, grab your walking shoes, your camera, and your sense of adventure, and let's explore this incredible city together!

Contents

1. Introduction

1.1 A Warm Welcome to Washington, D.C.

Welcome to the nation's capital, Washington, D.C.! A city rich in history, culture, and natural beauty, Washington, D.C., is a thriving metropolis that offers an unparalleled experience for visitors of all ages and interests. Home to iconic monuments, world-renowned museums, and diverse neighborhoods, the city is a treasure trove of attractions waiting to be discovered.

In this guide, we aim to provide you with an insider's perspective on the best that Washington, D.C., has to offer, ensuring that your trip is nothing short of unforgettable. From the bustling National Mall to the tranquil parks and gardens, our goal is to help you uncover the hidden gems and unique experiences that make Washington, D.C., truly special.

1.2 How to Use This Guide

To make the most of your time in Washington, D.C., this guide is organized into different sections, each focusing on a specific aspect of the city or a particular type of traveler. We recommend starting with the "Washington, D.C. at a Glance" section to gain a general understanding of the city's history, geography, culture, and cuisine. From there, you can dive into the sections that align best with your interests and travel preferences.

If you're looking for a comprehensive itinerary, explore the "Tailored Itineraries for Washington, D.C." section, which offers a range of trip plans based on various themes, trip durations, and travel styles. Each itinerary includes detailed day-by-day plans, including recommendations for attractions, dining, and entertainment options.

Throughout the guide, we've also included insider tips, practical information, and helpful resources to make your trip planning easier and more enjoyable. Whether you're a first-time visitor or a seasoned traveler, this guide will help you navigate Washington, D.C., with ease and confidence, leaving you with memories that will last a lifetime.

So, let's get started on your adventure through the heart of the United States – Washington, D.C.!

2. Washington, D.C. at a Glance

2.1 The Capital's Rich History

Established by the United States Constitution in 1790, Washington, D.C., serves as the capital of the United States and a symbol of the nation's democratic values. The city's unique history is inextricably linked with the country's founding principles and its evolution over time.

Washington, D.C., was strategically positioned along the Potomac River, with land donated by the states of Maryland and Virginia. Under the direction of President George Washington, French architect Pierre Charles L'Enfant designed the city's original layout, which features wide avenues, public squares, and grand buildings. The capital was officially named in honor of George Washington, while the "D.C." in its name represents the "District of Columbia," a special federal district created to house the capital separate from any state's jurisdiction.

Over the years, Washington, D.C., has witnessed some of the most defining moments in American history. From the swearing-in of presidents and the signing of landmark legislation to the organization of social movements and the celebration of national milestones, the city has been at the center of the nation's political and cultural life.

Today, Washington, D.C., is a living museum of American history, with countless monuments, memorials, and museums dedicated to preserving the nation's heritage. From the iconic Washington Monument and the Lincoln Memorial to the National Archives and the Library of Congress, the capital offers visitors an unparalleled opportunity to delve into the nation's past and reflect on its future.

As you explore the city, take the time to appreciate the rich history embedded in every corner of Washington, D.C. Whether you're strolling through the historic neighborhoods, participating in a guided tour, or simply admiring the architectural marvels, you'll find that the capital's history is an integral part of its enduring charm and allure.

2.2 Geography and Climate

Washington, D.C., is situated along the banks of the Potomac River, bordered by the states of Maryland to the northeast and Virginia to the southwest. The city's unique geography offers a mix of urban landscapes and lush green spaces, making it an ideal destination for both city explorers and nature lovers alike.

The District of Columbia spans roughly 68 square miles, with the Potomac River forming its natural western boundary. The city is divided into four quadrants – Northwest (NW), Northeast (NE), Southwest (SW), and Southeast (SE) – which converge at the U.S. Capitol building.

Washington, D.C., experiences a **humid subtropical climate**, characterized by hot, humid summers and cold, wet winters. Spring and fall are generally mild and pleasant, with the city's famous cherry blossoms drawing visitors from around the world each spring. The city's average temperature ranges from 37°F (3°C) in January to 79°F (26°C) in July. While snowfall is common during the winter months, severe snowstorms are relatively rare.

2.3 Culture and Lifestyle

Washington, D.C., is a **melting pot of cultures**, with residents hailing from various backgrounds and nationalities. This cultural diversity is reflected in the city's vibrant arts scene, lively neighborhoods, and diverse cuisine. D.C. is also home to a large diplomatic community, with more than 170 foreign embassies and numerous international organizations.

The city offers a rich array of **cultural and artistic experiences,** from world-class museums and galleries to thriving theaters and music venues. Washington, D.C., hosts numerous cultural festivals throughout the year, celebrating everything from jazz music and independent films to international cuisine and local artisans.

Washingtonians tend to lead **active lifestyles,** with many residents taking advantage of the city's abundant parks, trails, and recreational facilities. The city is known for its walkability and bike-friendliness, making it easy to explore its many sights and attractions on foot or by bicycle.

2.4 Culinary Scene

The diverse cultural landscape of Washington, D.C., is reflected in its **dynamic culinary scene.** From fine dining establishments and trendy eateries to food trucks and historic markets, the city offers a smorgasbord of flavors to satisfy every palate.

Washington, D.C., is particularly renowned for its **international cuisine,** with a wide array of restaurants serving dishes from around the world. From Ethiopian fare in Adams Morgan to authentic Vietnamese cuisine in Eden Center, the city's dining scene provides a global culinary tour for food enthusiasts.

In recent years, the city's food scene has embraced **sustainable and farm-to-table dining**, with many restaurants sourcing ingredients from local farms and producers. The city is also home to a burgeoning craft beverage scene, featuring microbreweries, distilleries, and wineries that showcase the region's rich agricultural heritage.

Don't forget to try some of the city's iconic dishes, such as the **D.C. half-smoke** – a local sausage specialty – and the **Chesapeake Bay blue crab**. These culinary experiences offer a taste of Washington, D.C.'s unique regional flavors and traditions.

3. Getting Around Washington, D.C.

3.1 Navigating the Public Transportation System

Washington, D.C., boasts a comprehensive public transportation system, making it easy and convenient for visitors to explore the city. The **Washington Metropolitan Area Transit Authority (WMATA)** operates the Metrorail and Metrobus systems, which cover the District and its surrounding suburbs.

The **Metrorail** system consists of six color-coded lines, serving 91 stations throughout the D.C. metropolitan area. The trains run from 5 a.m. to midnight on weekdays, and from 7 a.m. to midnight on weekends. Farecards can be purchased at any Metrorail station, with prices varying based on the distance traveled.

The **Metrobus** network complements the Metrorail system, providing extensive coverage across the city and its suburbs. Buses generally run from 5 a.m. to midnight, with some routes offering extended night service. Fares can be paid in cash, or by using a SmarTrip card, which also works on the Metrorail system.

3.2 Best Practices for Biking and Walking

Washington, D.C., is a **walkable and bike-friendly city**, with many attractions located within a short distance of one another. The city offers a vast network of sidewalks, bike lanes, and multi-use trails, making it easy for visitors to navigate on foot or by bicycle.

The **Capital Bikeshare** program allows visitors to rent bicycles for short trips around the city. With over 600 stations and thousands of bikes available, the system provides a convenient and affordable transportation option. Helmets are not provided, so it's a good idea to bring your own for safety.

When walking or biking in the city, be mindful of traffic signals and crosswalks, and always yield to pedestrians when cycling. It's also essential to lock up your bike securely to prevent theft.

3.3 Car Rentals, Taxis, and Rideshares

While public transportation is the most convenient way to get around Washington, D.C., visitors may choose to rent a car, hail a taxi, or use rideshare services like Uber or Lyft. Keep in mind that **parking can be limited and expensive** in the city, particularly around popular attractions.

Taxis and rideshare services are widely available throughout the city and can be a convenient option for short trips or when traveling with luggage. Be sure to factor in additional fees, such as airport surcharges, when using these services.

3.4 Accessibility Tips for Travelers

Washington, D.C., is committed to providing a welcoming and accessible experience for all visitors. Most attractions, museums, and public spaces offer wheelchair-accessible entrances, restrooms, and exhibits. The Metrorail and Metrobus systems also provide accommodations for individuals with disabilities, such as priority seating, visual and audible announcements, and accessible station entrances.

For visitors who require additional assistance or accommodations, it's a good idea to contact attractions and venues in advance to ensure a smooth and enjoyable experience.

When planning your visit, consider using resources like the D.C. Mayor's Office on Disability Rights and the Accessible Guide to Washington, D.C. These resources offer valuable information on accessibility features, services, and tips for navigating the city with ease.

3.5 How to Get from the Airport to the Center of Washington DC

Depending on which Airport you arrive at, you have different options for getting to the center of the city.

Dulles Airport (IAD)

Dulles Airport is 42 km west of downtown Washington, so the taxi option becomes rather expensive due to the long distance (between $60 and $80). Metrobus offers a service between the airport and downtown with the 5A bus. It's $7 that can be paid with cash, and the bus departs every 30 minutes or every hour depending on the day.

Another option is to take a shuttle service, which is more expensive than the metro bus but has the advantage that it will get you to your exact destination within the city. Super Shuttle offers service at $30 for the first passenger and $10 for each additional passenger, so if you're traveling in a large group, it may not be a bad option.

Ronald Reagan Airport (DCA)

Ronald Reagan Airport is only 5 km south of downtown Washington, so if you're arriving here everything is much easier.

The MetroRail conveniently connects Ronald Reagan Airport with the city, so this might be the best option. If you arrive at terminals B or C, then you can just walk to the MetroRail station, and if you arrive at the A terminal you can take any Airport Shuttle that will take you to terminals B or C. You may take the blue or yellow lines to get from the airport to wherever you want within DC. The maximum fare to any station of the metro system is $6.

4. Iconic Landmarks and Monuments

Washington, D.C., is a city steeped in history and filled with awe-inspiring landmarks and monuments that showcase the nation's heritage. From the famous structures lining the National Mall to lesser-known memorials tucked away in the city's neighborhoods, these sites offer visitors a chance to learn about and reflect on the people, events, and ideals that have shaped the United States.

4.1 The National Mall and Its Surroundings

The National Mall is the heart of Washington, D.C., and home to many of the city's most iconic landmarks and monuments. This two-mile-long stretch of green space is bordered by the U.S. Capitol building to the east and the Lincoln Memorial to the west, and offers visitors a breathtaking journey through the nation's history.

- **The U.S. Capitol:** The centerpiece of the National Mall, the U.S. Capitol is home to the U.S. Congress and a symbol of American democracy. Visitors can take a guided tour of the historic building, which includes stops at the Crypt, the Rotunda, and National Statuary Hall. The Capitol Visitor Center offers educational exhibits and resources, making it a must-see destination for history buffs.
- **The Washington Monument:** This towering obelisk, dedicated to the nation's first president, George Washington, stands at a height of 555 feet and offers panoramic views of the city from its observation deck. Visitors can reserve tickets in advance to ride the elevator to the top and enjoy the stunning vista.
- **The Lincoln Memorial:** Dedicated to the 16th president, Abraham Lincoln, this grand neoclassical monument is an iconic symbol of freedom and unity. The statue of Lincoln sits in a contemplative pose, surrounded by inscriptions of his Gettysburg Address and Second Inaugural Address, both of which underscore the importance of equality and liberty.

- **The World War II Memorial:** This expansive memorial honors the 16 million Americans who served in World War II, as well as the millions who supported the war effort on the home front. The memorial features 56 granite pillars representing U.S. states and territories and a reflecting pool, offering a serene space for reflection and remembrance.
- **The Vietnam Veterans Memorial:** Designed by architect Maya Lin, this poignant memorial consists of two black granite walls inscribed with the names of over 58,000 Americans who served and died in the Vietnam War. The simplicity and solemnity of the design evoke a sense of loss and honor for those who made the ultimate sacrifice.
- **The Thomas Jefferson Memorial:** This domed monument, inspired by the Roman Pantheon, honors the third U.S. president and author of the Declaration of Independence. The interior features a bronze statue of Jefferson, surrounded by excerpts from his writings, highlighting his enduring contributions to the country's founding principles.
- **The Martin Luther King Jr. Memorial:** Located near the Tidal Basin, this powerful memorial pays tribute to the civil rights leader and his vision of equality and justice. The centerpiece is a 30-foot-tall statue of King emerging from a "Stone of Hope," symbolizing his perseverance in the face of adversity.

4.2 Off-the-Beaten-Path Monuments and Memorials

While the National Mall boasts many of Washington, D.C.'s most famous monuments and memorials, venturing beyond the well-trodden path can lead to some truly remarkable and lesser-known sites. Here are some off-the-beaten-path monuments and memorials that you shouldn't miss during your visit to the capital.

1. Albert Einstein Memorial: Located on the grounds of the National Academy of Sciences, the Albert Einstein Memorial features a life-size bronze statue of the renowned physicist seated with his manuscripts. Surrounding the statue is a celestial map embedded in the pavement, representing the universe as it appeared on the date of the memorial's dedication.

2. Theodore Roosevelt Island: This tranquil island park in the Potomac River pays tribute to the 26th president of the United States, Theodore Roosevelt. The park features a memorial plaza with a bronze statue of Roosevelt, as well as numerous walking trails and peaceful wooded areas that showcase the president's passion for conservation and nature.

3. The United States National Arboretum: While primarily known for its extensive gardens and plant collections, the U.S. National Arboretum is also home to the National Capitol Columns. These 22 Corinthian sandstone columns once supported the east portico of the U.S. Capitol but were relocated to the arboretum in the 1980s. Set amidst lush greenery, the columns provide a unique and picturesque backdrop for visitors.

4. The Titanic Memorial: This simple yet evocative memorial is dedicated to the men who lost their lives during the Titanic disaster in 1912. The statue of a male figure with arms outstretched stands along the waterfront in Southwest Washington, D.C., symbolizing the sacrifice of those who gave their lives so that others might survive.

5. The District of Columbia War Memorial: This lesser-known memorial, located on the National Mall, commemorates the residents of the District of Columbia who served in World War I. The elegant domed structure, constructed of Vermont marble, is surrounded by a grove of trees, creating a peaceful and contemplative atmosphere.

6. The Korean War Veterans Memorial: Situated just south of the Lincoln Memorial Reflecting Pool, the Korean War Veterans Memorial honors those who served in the Korean War. The memorial consists of 19 stainless steel statues representing a squad on patrol, as well as a black granite wall etched with the faces of service members. The memorial's Pool of Remembrance provides a serene space for reflection.

7. The Franciscan Monastery of the Holy Land in America: This hidden gem in Washington, D.C.'s Brookland neighborhood offers a peaceful retreat from the bustling city. The Monastery features replicas of several Holy Land shrines, including the Grotto of Gethsemane and the Chapel of the Ascension. The Monastery's beautifully landscaped grounds include a rose garden, a meditation garden, and a Lourdes grotto.

Exploring these off-the-beaten-path monuments and memorials will enrich your visit to Washington, D.C., providing a deeper understanding of the city's history and the diverse stories it has to tell. Whether you're a history buff, an art enthusiast, or simply seeking a quieter experience away from the crowds, these lesser-known sites offer unique perspectives and memorable experiences.

4.3 Guided Tours: Historical, Cultural, and Thematic

Guided tours are an excellent way to explore Washington, D.C., offering expert insights into the city's rich history, vibrant culture, and unique attractions. From historical walking tours to thematic experiences, there's a tour to suit every interest. Here are some of the most popular and engaging guided tours available in the capital.

1. National Mall and Monument Tours: Several companies and organizations offer guided tours of the National Mall and its surrounding monuments, providing in-depth information on the history and significance of each site. Choose from walking tours, bike tours, or even Segway tours to cover more ground. Some tours focus specifically on the monuments at night, offering a breathtaking view of the illuminated landmarks.

2. Capitol Hill and U.S. Capitol Tours: Dive into the heart of American politics with a guided tour of Capitol Hill and the U.S. Capitol building. Learn about the legislative process, explore the stunning architecture, and discover the history of this iconic area. Some tours also include visits to the Library of Congress and the Supreme Court, providing a comprehensive look at the nation's government institutions.

3. Smithsonian Institution Tours: The Smithsonian Institution offers a variety of guided tours that showcase the best of its vast museum collections. Join a docent-led tour for expert insights into the highlights of the National Museum of American History, the National Museum of Natural History, or the National Air and Space Museum, among others.

4. Historic Neighborhood Tours: Explore Washington, D.C.'s diverse neighborhoods with guided walking tours that delve into the history and culture of each area. Discover the rich heritage of Georgetown, the vibrant street art of Adams Morgan, or the stunning architecture of Embassy Row. Each neighborhood offers a unique perspective on the city's storied past and present.

5. African American History and Culture Tours: Washington, D.C., has a deep-rooted African American history, which can be explored through specialized guided tours. Visit important landmarks such as the African American Civil War Memorial, the Martin Luther King Jr. Memorial, and historic neighborhoods like U Street and Anacostia. Many tours also include a visit to the National Museum of African American History and Culture.

6. Ghost and Haunted History Tours: For those interested in the spookier side of Washington, D.C., ghost and haunted history tours offer an intriguing look into the city's paranormal past. Hear tales of ghosts, unsolved mysteries, and eerie events as you explore haunted locations such as the Old Stone House, the Octagon House, and the Capitol building.

7. Food and Culinary Tours: Discover the capital's diverse culinary scene with a guided food tour that takes you to some of the city's best eateries, markets, and hidden gems. Sample regional specialties, international cuisine, and local favorites while learning about the history and culture that influence Washington, D.C.'s vibrant food scene.

8. Thematic and Specialty Tours: Washington, D.C., offers an array of specialty tours catering to specific interests, such as art and architecture, espionage and spy history, presidential history, or women's history. These thematic tours provide an in-depth exploration of a particular topic, offering a unique and engaging way to experience the city.

No matter your interests or passions, guided tours in Washington, D.C., provide an enriching and educational way to delve deeper into the city.

5.Museums and Cultural Institutions

5.1 The Smithsonian Institution and Its Museums

The Smithsonian Institution, often referred to as "the nation's attic," is a collection of 19 museums, galleries, and a zoo, making it the world's largest museum, education, and research complex. Most of the Smithsonian museums are located in Washington, D.C., and offer free admission to the public. Here are some of the most prominent Smithsonian museums and galleries in the city:

1. National Museum of American History: This museum houses a vast collection of artifacts and exhibits that chronicle the history of the United States, from the founding of the nation to present day. Key highlights include the original Star-Spangled Banner, the First Ladies' Inaugural Gowns, and the Greensboro lunch counter from the Civil Rights Movement.

2. National Air and Space Museum: Celebrating the history of aviation and space exploration, the National Air and Space Museum is one of the most visited museums in the world. The museum's collection includes the Wright brothers' 1903 Flyer, Charles Lindbergh's Spirit of St. Louis, and the Apollo 11 Command Module Columbia.

3. National Museum of Natural History: This museum offers visitors a fascinating journey through the natural world, from prehistoric times to the present day. The museum features extensive exhibits on dinosaurs, mammals, geology, and ocean life, as well as the iconic Hope Diamond.

4. National Gallery of Art: The National Gallery of Art consists of two buildings – the West Building, which focuses on European and American art from the 13th to the early 20th century, and the East Building, which houses modern and contemporary art. The museum's collection includes masterpieces by artists such as Leonardo da Vinci, Rembrandt, and Jackson Pollock.

5. Hirshhorn Museum and Sculpture Garden: Dedicated to contemporary art and culture, the Hirshhorn Museum features an impressive collection of paintings, sculptures, and mixed-media works from the 20th and 21st centuries. The museum's distinctive cylindrical building and outdoor sculpture garden make it a must-visit destination for art enthusiasts.

6. National Museum of African American History and Culture: This museum, which opened in 2016, is the newest addition to the Smithsonian Institution. It explores the rich and diverse history of African Americans, from the early days of the transatlantic slave trade to the Civil Rights Movement and beyond. The museum's powerful exhibits and interactive displays offer an immersive and thought-provoking experience.

7. National Museum of the American Indian: This museum celebrates the history, culture, and contributions of Native peoples from across the Western Hemisphere. With a focus on storytelling, the museum features engaging exhibits, art, and artifacts that showcase the diverse traditions and experiences of indigenous communities.

8. Smithsonian Institution Building (The Castle): Serving as the institution's information center, the Castle is an excellent starting point for your Smithsonian adventure. The building itself is a beautiful example of 19th-century Gothic Revival architecture and houses temporary exhibits, the Smithsonian Visitor Center, and the institution's administrative offices.

These are just a few of the many Smithsonian museums and galleries available to explore in Washington, D.C. Each offers a unique and enriching experience, providing insight into the nation's history, culture, and artistic achievements. Whether you're interested in art, science, or history, the Smithsonian Institution has something for everyone.

Smithsonian Museum / Gallery	Website	Open Hours	Ticket Price
National Museum of American History	americanhistory.si.edu	10 a.m. – 5:30 p.m. daily	Free
National Air and Space Museum	airandspace.si.edu	10 a.m. – 5:30 p.m. daily	Free
National Museum of Natural History	naturalhistory.si.edu	10 a.m. – 5:30 p.m. daily	Free
National Gallery of Art (West Building and East Building)	nga.gov	10 a.m. – 5 p.m. daily	Free
Hirshhorn Museum and Sculpture Garden	hirshhorn.si.edu	10 a.m. – 5:30 p.m. daily	Free
National Museum of African American History and Culture	nmaahc.si.edu	10 a.m. – 5:30 p.m. daily	Free
National Museum of the American Indian	americanindian.si.edu	10 a.m. – 5:30 p.m. daily	Free
Smithsonian Institution Building (The Castle)	si.edu/visit	8:30 a.m. – 5:30 p.m. daily	Free

Please note that open hours and other information may change over time or due to special circumstances. It is always a good idea to check the museum's website for the most up-to-date information before planning your visit.

5.2 Lesser-Known Museums and Galleries

In addition to the world-renowned Smithsonian museums, Washington, D.C. is home to a variety of lesser-known museums and galleries that cater to a wide range of interests. These hidden gems offer unique experiences and opportunities for cultural enrichment, often with smaller crowds and more intimate settings. Here are some noteworthy lesser-known museums and galleries in the city:

1. The Phillips Collection: Established in 1921, The Phillips Collection is America's first museum of modern art. Located in the Dupont Circle neighborhood, this museum features an impressive collection of European and American masterpieces, including works by Renoir, Rothko, and O'Keeffe. The museum's intimate atmosphere and rotating exhibitions make it a favorite among art enthusiasts.

2. International Spy Museum: This museum provides a fascinating look into the world of espionage, showcasing the history and tools of the trade. With interactive exhibits, artifacts, and stories of real spies, the International Spy Museum offers an intriguing and educational experience for visitors of all ages.

3. National Museum of Women in the Arts: As the only major museum in the world dedicated solely to women artists, the National Museum of Women in the Arts showcases a diverse collection of works spanning various time periods and artistic styles. The museum's mission is to celebrate the achievements of women artists and inspire future generations.

4. Newseum (reopening in 2023): Although temporarily closed, the Newseum is a unique museum dedicated to the history and importance of a free press. The museum features exhibits that explore the evolution of news, journalism, and the First Amendment. The Newseum's reopening is anticipated in 2023 at a new location.

5. The Kreeger Museum: Housed in a striking mid-century modern residence, The Kreeger Museum features the private collection of David and Carmen Kreeger. The museum includes works by prominent artists such as Picasso, Monet, and Rodin, as well as a sculpture garden and rotating exhibitions.

6. The National Building Museum: This museum celebrates the history and impact of architecture, design, and urban planning. The National Building Museum's exhibits and programs explore the built environment and its role in shaping our lives, communities, and cities.

7. The National Museum of Health and Medicine: This lesser-known museum, located just outside of Washington, D.C., showcases the history of medicine and its advancements. With exhibits ranging from Civil War-era surgical tools to modern prosthetics, the National Museum of Health and Medicine provides a fascinating insight into the development of medical practices and technologies.

These lesser-known museums and galleries in Washington, D.C., offer a wealth of opportunities to expand your cultural horizons and explore new interests. Whether you're interested in art, history, or science, there's a hidden gem waiting to be discovered.

5.3 Performing Arts Venues

Washington, D.C. boasts a vibrant performing arts scene, offering a diverse array of venues and performances to cater to various tastes and interests. From world-class theater and dance to local music and comedy, the city has something for everyone. Here are some of the most prominent performing arts venues in Washington, D.C.:

1. The John F. Kennedy Center for the Performing Arts: As the nation's premier performing arts center, the Kennedy Center hosts a wide range of performances, including theater, dance, orchestral music, and opera. The center is home to the National Symphony Orchestra, Washington National Opera, and the Suzanne Farrell Ballet. The Kennedy Center also offers free daily performances on its Millennium Stage, featuring a mix of local, national, and international artists.

2. Ford's Theatre: Steeped in history, Ford's Theatre is where President Abraham Lincoln was assassinated in 1865. Today, the theater operates as a working performance venue, hosting a variety of plays and musicals that celebrate the American experience. The theater also houses a museum and education center, offering a unique blend of history and live performances.

3. Arena Stage: Arena Stage is one of the oldest and most respected regional theaters in the country. Known for producing high-quality American plays and musicals, Arena Stage has helped launch the careers of numerous playwrights and actors. The theater's modern, waterfront location in the Southwest Waterfront neighborhood adds to its appeal.

4. The Shakespeare Theatre Company: This award-winning theater company is dedicated to producing the works of William Shakespeare and other classic playwrights. With performances held at the Lansburgh Theatre and Sidney Harman Hall, the Shakespeare Theatre Company offers a mix of traditional and innovative interpretations of classic plays, often featuring renowned actors and directors.

5. Woolly Mammoth Theatre Company: Known for its innovative and thought-provoking productions, Woolly Mammoth Theatre Company is a leader in contemporary theater. The company focuses on presenting new plays and fostering the work of emerging playwrights, making it an excellent venue for those seeking cutting-edge theater experiences.

6. Warner Theatre: This historic theater, located in downtown Washington, D.C., hosts a variety of performances, including concerts, comedy shows, and dance performances. The Warner Theatre's elegant architecture and diverse programming make it a popular destination for entertainment in the city.

7. 9:30 Club: As one of D.C.'s most iconic music venues, the 9:30 Club has been a staple in the city's live music scene for decades. The club hosts a wide range of local, national, and international artists, spanning various genres, from rock and hip-hop to electronic and indie music.

8. The Anthem: Located in the Wharf development along the Southwest Waterfront, The Anthem is a relatively new addition to D.C.'s music scene. This state-of-the-art concert venue can accommodate up to 6,000 people and hosts a diverse lineup of artists and events, including major touring acts and local performers.

These performing arts venues are just a small sample of the cultural richness that Washington, D.C. has to offer. With numerous options to choose from, you're sure to find a performance that will captivate and inspire you during your visit to the nation's capital.

5.4 Workshops and Classes for Culture Enthusiasts

For those looking to immerse themselves in the rich cultural offerings of Washington, D.C., participating in workshops and classes is a fantastic way to engage with the local art scene and learn new skills. From hands-on art classes to dance lessons and cooking demonstrations, there is a wide variety of opportunities to expand your cultural horizons. Here are some popular workshops and classes for culture enthusiasts in Washington, D.C.:

1. ArtJamz Underground Studio: Unleash your inner artist at ArtJamz, a creative space where you can paint on canvas while sipping on your favorite beverage. The studio provides all the materials you'll need, and experienced instructors are available to guide you through the process, making it a fun and relaxing experience for artists of all levels.

2. Capitol Hill Arts Workshop (CHAW): CHAW offers a variety of art classes, including painting, drawing, ceramics, photography, and printmaking. With a focus on community and accessibility, the workshop provides a welcoming environment for artists of all ages and skill levels to explore their creativity.

3. Dance Place: Dance Place is a hub for dance education and performance in D.C., offering classes in various styles such as ballet, hip-hop, contemporary, and African dance. Whether you're a seasoned dancer or a complete beginner, Dance Place provides an inclusive and supportive atmosphere to learn and grow.

4. CulinAerie: This recreational cooking school offers hands-on cooking classes led by experienced chefs. From global cuisine to baking and pastry, CulinAerie's diverse class offerings cater to all skill levels and culinary interests. The school also offers wine and spirits tastings and team-building events.

5. The Writer's Center: If you're passionate about writing, The Writer's Center offers workshops and classes in various genres, including fiction, poetry, memoir, and screenwriting. The center's instructors are experienced writers and educators, providing guidance and support for aspiring writers in a nurturing environment.

6. Washington Photo Safari: Improve your photography skills by joining a Washington Photo Safari led by professional photographers. These guided tours offer practical, hands-on instruction while exploring some of D.C.'s most iconic locations. The safaris cater to all skill levels, from beginners to advanced photographers.

7. The Washington School of Ballet: Offering classes for both children and adults, The Washington School of Ballet provides high-quality instruction in classical ballet technique. The school's experienced instructors create a supportive environment that fosters artistic growth and development.

8. Hill Center at the Old Naval Hospital: This historic cultural center offers a diverse range of classes and workshops, including art, music, language, and cooking. With a focus on community engagement and lifelong learning, the Hill Center provides a welcoming space for individuals to explore new interests and develop their skills.

By participating in these workshops and classes, you'll not only have the opportunity to learn new skills and engage with Washington, D.C.'s vibrant cultural scene, but also connect with like-minded individuals who share your passions. Dive in and embrace the city's creative spirit!

6. Parks and Outdoor Activities

Washington, D.C. is a city blessed with an abundance of green spaces and outdoor recreational opportunities. With its well-maintained parks, picturesque trails, and scenic waterfront areas, the nation's capital offers a variety of ways to enjoy the outdoors and appreciate nature. Whether you're looking for a quiet respite from the bustling city or seeking adventurous outdoor activities, D.C. has something for everyone. In this chapter, we will explore some of the best parks and outdoor activities within the city and its surrounding areas.

6.1 Urban Oases: Parks within the City

Washington, D.C. is a city blessed with an abundance of green spaces and outdoor recreational opportunities. With its well-maintained parks, picturesque trails, and scenic waterfront areas, the nation's capital offers a variety of ways to enjoy the outdoors and appreciate nature. Whether you're looking for a quiet respite from the bustling city or seeking adventurous outdoor activities, D.C. has something for everyone. In this chapter, we will explore some of the best parks and outdoor activities within the city and its surrounding areas.

6.1 Urban Oases: Parks within the City

Dotted throughout Washington, D.C., numerous parks and green spaces provide residents and visitors with a chance to escape the city's hustle and bustle. These urban oases are perfect for picnics, leisurely strolls, or simply relaxing with a good book. Here are some of the most notable parks within the city:

1. **Rock Creek Park:** One of the largest urban parks in the country, Rock Creek Park spans over 1,700 acres and offers a range of activities, including hiking, biking, horseback riding, and even a planetarium. The park's winding trails, lush forests, and picturesque creek make it an ideal destination for nature lovers.

2. **Meridian Hill Park:** Also known as Malcolm X Park, Meridian Hill Park is a historic urban park that features a cascading fountain, statues, and beautifully landscaped terraces. This park is a popular spot for picnics, sunbathing, and community events, including the renowned Sunday drum circle.
3. **National Arboretum:** This 446-acre living museum showcases a wide variety of plants and trees, including the famous National Capitol Columns and the enchanting Bonsai and Penjing Museum. With its scenic walking trails and peaceful atmosphere, the National Arboretum is a favorite destination for plant enthusiasts and nature lovers alike.
4. **Georgetown Waterfront Park:** Situated along the Potomac River, Georgetown Waterfront Park offers stunning views of the river and the Kennedy Center. The park features walking and biking paths, grassy areas for picnicking, and a relaxing riverside ambiance.
5. **Theodore Roosevelt Island:** This secluded island park in the Potomac River is dedicated to the conservation-minded 26th president, Theodore Roosevelt. Accessible only by footbridge, the park offers a tranquil escape from the city, with wooded trails, a memorial plaza, and abundant wildlife.
6. **Dumbarton Oaks Park:** Nestled in the historic Georgetown neighborhood, Dumbarton Oaks Park is a hidden gem that features meandering paths, terraced gardens, and serene woodlands. The park is particularly beautiful in the springtime, when its cherry blossoms and azaleas are in full bloom.

These urban oases provide a welcome retreat from the fast pace of city life, offering residents and visitors alike the chance to unwind, connect with nature, and recharge their batteries.

6.2 Scenic Trails and Hiking Spots

Washington, D.C. and its surrounding areas are home to numerous scenic trails and hiking spots that cater to a wide range of fitness levels and preferences. From leisurely strolls to challenging hikes, these trails offer a fantastic opportunity to explore the region's natural beauty and enjoy some fresh air. Here are some of the most popular trails and hiking spots in and around Washington, D.C.:

1. **Capital Crescent Trail:** This 11-mile paved trail stretches from Georgetown to Silver Spring, Maryland, and is popular among walkers, joggers, cyclists, and inline skaters. The trail follows the path of a former railroad line and offers picturesque views of the Potomac River and the surrounding woodlands.

2. **C&O Canal Towpath:** The Chesapeake and Ohio Canal Towpath is a 184.5-mile trail that runs alongside the historic C&O Canal from Georgetown in Washington, D.C., to Cumberland, Maryland. The towpath is a favorite among hikers, cyclists, and history buffs, offering a glimpse into the region's past while traversing through diverse landscapes.

3. **Mount Vernon Trail:** This 18-mile multi-use trail runs parallel to the Potomac River, connecting Theodore Roosevelt Island to George Washington's Mount Vernon Estate. The trail offers stunning views of the Washington, D.C. skyline, wooded sections, and historic landmarks, making it a favorite for locals and visitors alike.

4. **Rock Creek Park Trails:** With over 32 miles of hiking trails within Rock Creek Park, there are plenty of options for nature lovers to explore. The Western Ridge Trail and the Valley Trail are two popular options, offering varying levels of difficulty and opportunities to spot local wildlife.

5. **Great Falls Park:** Located just outside of Washington, D.C., in Virginia, Great Falls Park is known for its spectacular views of

the Potomac River's rushing rapids and waterfalls. The park offers a range of trails, from the leisurely River Trail to the more challenging Billy Goat Trail, which requires some scrambling over rocks and steep terrain.

6. **Theodore Roosevelt Island Trails:** The island's 2.5-mile trail network winds through wooded areas and marshland, providing hikers with a peaceful and secluded experience. The Upland Trail and Swamp Trail offer differing views of the island's diverse ecosystems, while the boardwalk provides a unique perspective on the marsh habitat.

7. **Scott's Run Nature Preserve:** Situated along the Potomac River in nearby McLean, Virginia, Scott's Run Nature Preserve offers a network of trails through dense forests and steep terrain. The preserve's main attraction is its picturesque waterfall, accessible via a relatively short but rugged hike.

These scenic trails and hiking spots provide a perfect opportunity to escape the urban environment and immerse yourself in the region's natural beauty. Whether you're a seasoned hiker or just looking for a leisurely stroll, there's a trail waiting for you to explore.

6.3 Boating, Kayaking, and Paddleboarding

Washington, D.C. boasts numerous waterways, including the Potomac River, the Anacostia River, and the Tidal Basin, providing ample opportunities for boating, kayaking, and paddleboarding. These water-based activities offer a unique perspective on the city and its surrounding landscapes while allowing you to enjoy some outdoor recreation. Here are some popular spots and rental facilities for boating, kayaking, and paddleboarding in the D.C. area:

1. **Key Bridge Boathouse:** Located in Georgetown, the Key Bridge Boathouse offers kayak, canoe, and stand-up paddleboard rentals. Paddle along the scenic Potomac River, taking in views of the Kennedy Center, the Watergate Complex, and the iconic D.C. skyline.

2. **Tidal Basin Paddle Boats:** For a leisurely boating experience with a touch of history, rent a paddleboat on the Tidal Basin. Glide across the water while enjoying up-close views of the Jefferson Memorial, Martin Luther King Jr. Memorial, and the beautiful cherry blossom trees during peak bloom.

3. **Ballpark Boathouse:** Situated near Nationals Park, the Ballpark Boathouse offers kayak and canoe rentals, allowing you to explore the Anacostia River. Paddle through the tranquil Anacostia Riverwalk Trail, or venture to Kingman and Heritage Islands for a unique urban wildlife experience.

4. **The Wharf Boathouse:** Located at the Southwest Waterfront, The Wharf Boathouse rents kayaks and paddleboards for use on the Washington Channel. Paddle past landmarks such as East Potomac Park, Hains Point, and Fort McNair while enjoying views of the bustling waterfront district.

5. **Fletcher's Boathouse:** Nestled along the C&O Canal, Fletcher's Boathouse offers rowboat, canoe, kayak, and paddleboard rentals. Take a leisurely paddle along the canal or venture into the Potomac River to enjoy the serene natural beauty of the area.

6. **Thompson Boat Center:** Situated near the Georgetown waterfront, the Thompson Boat Center rents kayaks, canoes, and paddleboards, as well as bikes for those who wish to explore the nearby trails. Paddle upriver to experience the stunning beauty of the Potomac River Gorge or take in the sights of the D.C. skyline as you glide downstream.

7. **Bladensburg Waterfront Park:** Located just outside of Washington, D.C., in Maryland, Bladensburg Waterfront Park offers canoe, kayak, and paddleboard rentals for exploring the Anacostia River. Discover the area's rich history and diverse wildlife as you paddle through the peaceful waterways.

Whether you're an experienced paddler or a beginner looking for a new way to enjoy the outdoors, Washington, D.C.'s waterways provide a fantastic setting for boating, kayaking, and paddleboarding. Soak up the sun, enjoy the views, and experience the city from a unique vantage point.

6.4 Wildlife Encounters and Conservation Areas

Washington, D.C. and its surrounding areas offer numerous opportunities to observe and appreciate local wildlife and natural habitats. From birdwatching to exploring conservation areas, these experiences provide a chance to learn about the region's biodiversity and the importance of preserving it. Here are some top wildlife encounters and conservation areas in and around the nation's capital:

1. **Kenilworth Park and Aquatic Gardens:** This hidden gem in Northeast D.C. is home to various species of waterfowl, turtles, and other aquatic creatures. Explore the boardwalk trails through the marsh, marvel at the aquatic gardens' blooming water lilies and lotus flowers, and keep an eye out for the park's resident beaver population.
2. **Rock Creek Park Nature Center and Planetarium:** The Nature Center at Rock Creek Park offers educational exhibits, live animal displays, and guided nature walks. Learn about the park's diverse wildlife, including deer, foxes, and over 200 species of birds, while exploring the park's tranquil forests and meadows.

3. **National Zoo:** Part of the Smithsonian Institution, the National Zoo is home to over 2,700 animals representing more than 390 species. The zoo's exhibits focus on conservation and education, showcasing animals such as giant pandas, elephants, and cheetahs in naturalistic habitats.
4. **Dyke Marsh Wildlife Preserve:** Located along the Potomac River in Virginia, Dyke Marsh Wildlife Preserve is one of the largest remaining freshwater tidal wetlands in the region. The preserve offers birdwatching and nature walks, with opportunities to spot bald eagles, ospreys, herons, and other waterfowl.
5. **Huntley Meadows Park:** Situated in Alexandria, Virginia, Huntley Meadows Park is a 1,500-acre wetland habitat that serves as a sanctuary for diverse wildlife. Explore the park's boardwalk trails, watch for beavers and muskrats, and enjoy the sight of colorful dragonflies and butterflies.
6. **Patuxent Research Refuge:** Established in 1936, Patuxent Research Refuge in Maryland is the nation's only National Wildlife Refuge dedicated to wildlife research. With over 12,000 acres of diverse habitats, the refuge offers ample opportunities for wildlife observation, photography, and environmental education.
7. **Meadowlark Botanical Gardens:** Located in Vienna, Virginia, Meadowlark Botanical Gardens is a 95-acre site dedicated to the cultivation and preservation of native plants and their habitats. Stroll through the gardens and woodlands to discover a wide range of flora and fauna, including turtles, frogs, and various bird species.

These wildlife encounters and conservation areas provide valuable opportunities to learn about the region's diverse ecosystems and the importance of preserving them for future generations. Enjoy the beauty of nature while gaining a deeper appreciation for the delicate balance of our environment.

7. Shopping and Entertainment

7.1 Distinctive Neighborhoods and Shopping Districts

Washington, D.C.'s vibrant shopping scene reflects its diverse neighborhoods and rich cultural history. From upscale boutiques to quirky local shops, the city's shopping districts offer something for everyone. Here are some of the most distinctive neighborhoods and shopping districts in Washington, D.C.:

1. **Georgetown:** This historic neighborhood, characterized by its charming cobblestone streets and Federal-style architecture, boasts a mix of high-end retailers, independent boutiques, and antique shops. Stroll along M Street and Wisconsin Avenue to discover trendy fashion stores, specialty shops, and unique gift items.

2. **Dupont Circle:** Known for its lively atmosphere and cultural institutions, Dupont Circle is home to a range of shops, from independent bookstores to art galleries. Browse Connecticut Avenue for upscale clothing boutiques and local artisans' creations, or visit the Dupont Circle Farmers Market for fresh produce and handmade goods.

3. **14th Street and U Street Corridor:** This rapidly evolving district is fast becoming a destination for fashion-forward shoppers. Explore the area's mix of vintage stores, designer boutiques, and home decor shops, along with a lively nightlife scene, including bars, music venues, and theaters.

4. **Eastern Market:** Located in the historic Capitol Hill neighborhood, Eastern Market is a vibrant public market featuring fresh produce, flowers, handmade crafts, and antiques. On weekends, the market expands to include local artisans and vendors selling a variety of unique items, from handmade jewelry to custom artwork.

5. **CityCenterDC:** This upscale, mixed-use development in the heart of downtown D.C. offers a luxurious shopping experience. Browse

high-end fashion brands, designer boutiques, and specialty stores, or dine at one of the many chic restaurants and cafes that line the pedestrian-friendly streets.

6. **Union Market:** This revitalized industrial area has transformed into a thriving food and retail destination. The indoor market features a variety of artisan food vendors, while the surrounding neighborhood is home to unique shops, art galleries, and local craft breweries.

7. **Adams Morgan:** Known for its eclectic vibe, Adams Morgan is a great destination for those in search of vintage clothing, unique gifts, and international wares. Wander along 18th Street and Columbia Road to discover a variety of specialty shops, record stores, and independent bookstores.

8. **The Wharf:** This modern waterfront district is a lively destination for shopping, dining, and entertainment. Browse the shops along the promenade for clothing, accessories, and gifts, or take in a show at one of the area's concert venues and theaters.

Each of these distinctive neighborhoods and shopping districts offers a unique shopping experience, reflecting the diverse culture and history of Washington, D.C. Whether you're in search of designer fashion or locally crafted treasures, you're sure to find the perfect items to suit your taste and budget.

7.2 Local Boutiques and Artisanal Finds

Washington, D.C. is home to a thriving community of local artists, designers, and craftspeople, whose creations can be found in charming boutiques and artisanal shops throughout the city. These establishments showcase the creativity and talent of the local community and offer a unique shopping experience for those seeking one-of-a-kind items. Here are some noteworthy local boutiques and artisanal finds in the nation's capital:

1. **Salt & Sundry:** This stylish boutique, with locations in Union Market and Logan Circle, features a carefully curated selection of home goods, gifts, and accessories. Browse handcrafted ceramics, artisanal candles, and distinctive textiles that reflect the store's modern, bohemian aesthetic.
2. **Miss Pixie's Furnishings & Whatnot:** Located in the bustling 14th Street corridor, Miss Pixie's is a treasure trove of vintage furniture, quirky home accessories, and eclectic decor. The constantly rotating inventory ensures that each visit to this beloved shop offers a fresh and exciting experience.
3. **Stitch & Rivet:** This artisan leather goods studio in Brookland offers a range of handmade bags, wallets, and accessories, crafted with high-quality materials and designed for longevity. Each piece is thoughtfully created to combine style, function, and durability.
4. **Cherry Blossom Creative:** Located in the heart of Shaw, Cherry Blossom Creative is a design studio and retail space featuring locally-made art prints, stationery, and gifts. The shop also offers custom design services, including branding, wedding invitations, and more.
5. **Curio Concept Store:** Situated in Georgetown, Curio Concept Store is a fashion-forward boutique showcasing an eclectic mix of emerging designers, avant-garde apparel, and unique accessories. This carefully curated shop is an excellent destination for those seeking statement pieces and cutting-edge styles.
6. **The Outrage:** This socially-conscious boutique in Adams Morgan offers apparel, accessories, and gifts designed to empower and inspire. With a focus on women's rights and social justice, The Outrage donates a portion of its proceeds to various nonprofit organizations.
7. **Made in DC:** As the name suggests, Made in DC is a retail space dedicated to showcasing products designed, crafted, or built in the nation's capital. Located in Dupont Circle, the shop features a

rotating selection of goods from local artisans, including jewelry, home decor, and gourmet food items.

8. **Shop Made in DC:** With locations in Georgetown, The Wharf, and Downtown, Shop Made in DC is a collective retail space that highlights the work of local makers and artists. Discover handcrafted jewelry, unique home goods, and creative gifts, all made by talented D.C. residents.

These local boutiques and artisanal shops offer a unique opportunity to explore the creativity and craftsmanship of Washington, D.C.'s thriving arts community. By shopping at these establishments, you not only support local businesses but also contribute to the vibrant and dynamic culture that makes the city so special.

7.3 Live Music and Nightlife

Washington, D.C.'s lively music scene and diverse nightlife options make it an exciting destination for evening entertainment. From intimate jazz clubs to historic music venues, and from vibrant rooftop bars to laid-back pubs, the city offers a wide range of options to suit every taste. Here are some top picks for live music and nightlife in Washington, D.C.:

1. **9:30 Club:** This iconic venue, located in the U Street Corridor, has been a staple of D.C.'s music scene for decades. Known for hosting both established and up-and-coming artists from various genres, the 9:30 Club offers an intimate concert experience and consistently draws enthusiastic crowds.

2. **Blues Alley:** Nestled in Georgetown, Blues Alley is the city's oldest continuously operating jazz and supper club. Enjoy live performances from local and international jazz artists while dining

on a menu inspired by New Orleans cuisine in this intimate, historic venue.

3. **The Anthem:** Located at The Wharf, The Anthem is a state-of-the-art music venue that hosts a diverse array of concerts, from rock and indie to hip-hop and electronic acts. With a spacious interior and excellent acoustics, The Anthem has quickly become a favorite among music lovers.

4. **Black Cat:** This indie rock venue in the 14th Street and U Street Corridor has been a fixture of the D.C. music scene since the 1990s. With two stages and a laid-back atmosphere, Black Cat showcases local and touring bands, as well as hosting dance parties and special events.

5. **The Hamilton Live:** Situated near the White House, The Hamilton Live is an elegant, multi-level venue featuring live music, fine dining, and a sophisticated lounge area. The venue hosts a variety of artists across genres, from jazz and blues to rock and folk.

6. **Echostage:** As the largest dedicated concert venue in D.C., Echostage offers an immersive experience for fans of electronic dance music, hip-hop, and pop. With state-of-the-art sound and lighting systems, this expansive venue in Northeast D.C. regularly hosts top DJs and performers from around the world.

7. **DC9 Nightclub:** This intimate venue in the U Street Corridor is a favorite for live indie music, DJ sets, and dance parties. With a rooftop bar offering stunning city views, DC9 Nightclub is a great spot to unwind and enjoy D.C.'s vibrant nightlife.

8. **The Howard Theatre:** A historic landmark in Shaw, The Howard Theatre has been hosting live performances since 1910. After an extensive renovation, this legendary venue continues to feature a diverse lineup of musicians, comedians, and other performers in an elegant setting.

9. **Barmini:** For a unique cocktail experience, head to Barmini, a modernist cocktail lab located in Penn Quarter. This intimate and

innovative bar offers an extensive menu of creative drinks, with expert mixologists crafting visually stunning concoctions.

7.4 Annual Festivals and Special Events

Washington, D.C. hosts a variety of annual festivals and special events throughout the year, celebrating the city's diverse culture, rich history, and vibrant arts scene. From seasonal celebrations to music, food, and film festivals, these events provide unique experiences for residents and visitors alike. Here are some of the most notable annual events in the nation's capital:

1. **National Cherry Blossom Festival:** Held each spring (usually late March to early April), this iconic festival commemorates the friendship between the United States and Japan and celebrates the beautiful cherry blossoms that grace the city. The festival includes a parade, cultural performances, and numerous special events throughout the city.
2. **Smithsonian Folklife Festival:** Taking place each summer on the National Mall, the Smithsonian Folklife Festival is a celebration of cultural heritage and traditions from around the world. The event features performances, demonstrations, workshops, and food from various countries and regions, showcasing the diversity of human culture.
3. **DC Jazz Festival:** Held annually in June, the DC Jazz Festival showcases the talents of local, national, and international jazz artists in venues across the city. The festival offers a mix of ticketed concerts and free performances, making it accessible to music lovers of all budgets.
4. **A Capitol Fourth:** This Independence Day celebration on the National Mall is a must-see event, featuring a free concert by the

National Symphony Orchestra, celebrity performers, and a spectacular fireworks display over the Washington Monument.

5. **DC Shorts Film Festival:** Taking place each September, the DC Shorts Film Festival highlights the work of independent filmmakers from around the world. The festival showcases short films in various genres, including narrative, documentary, and animation, as well as hosting panel discussions and filmmaker Q&A sessions.

6. **Taste of DC:** Held each October, Taste of DC is a food and drink festival that showcases the city's diverse culinary scene. Sample dishes from local restaurants, enjoy live music and cooking demonstrations, and explore the marketplace featuring local artisans and food vendors.

7. **National Christmas Tree Lighting Ceremony:** This annual event in early December marks the beginning of the holiday season in Washington, D.C. Held on the Ellipse, just south of the White House, the ceremony features live musical performances and the lighting of the National Christmas Tree.

8. **DC Emancipation Day:** Celebrated on April 16, this annual event commemorates the signing of the Compensated Emancipation Act by President Abraham Lincoln, which ended slavery in Washington, D.C. The day is marked by a parade, concerts, and educational events throughout the city.

These annual festivals and special events offer unique opportunities to engage with Washington, D.C.'s vibrant culture and diverse community. Whether you're a resident or a visitor, be sure to take part in these exciting events and make the most of your time in the nation's capital.

8. Food and Drink Experiences

8.1 Iconic D.C. Eateries and Food Traditions

8.1 Iconic D.C. Eateries and Food Traditions

Washington, D.C. is a culinary melting pot, offering a diverse range of dining experiences that reflect the city's rich history and multicultural heritage. From classic American fare to international flavors, here are some iconic D.C. eateries and food traditions you won't want to miss:

1. **Ben's Chili Bowl:** A D.C. institution since 1958, Ben's Chili Bowl is famous for its half-smoke sausages, chili dogs, and warm, welcoming atmosphere. Located at 1213 U St NW, Washington, D.C., this iconic eatery has been visited by countless celebrities and politicians over the years. Website: https://www.benschilibowl.com/; Average prices: $5-$15.

2. **Old Ebbitt Grill:** Established in 1856, Old Ebbitt Grill is the oldest dining saloon in Washington, D.C. Situated at 675 15th St NW, this historic restaurant serves classic American fare, including seafood, steaks, and an extensive raw bar selection. Website: https://www.ebbitt.com/; Average prices: $15-$40.

3. **Martin's Tavern:** Located at 1264 Wisconsin Ave NW, Martin's Tavern has been a Georgetown staple since 1933. Known for its cozy atmosphere and delicious comfort food, this classic eatery has hosted every U.S. president from Harry Truman to George W. Bush. Website: https://www.martinstavern.com/; Average prices: $15-$30.

4. **Mama Ayesha's:** Serving Middle Eastern cuisine since 1960, Mama Ayesha's offers a variety of traditional dishes, including falafel, hummus, and kebabs. Located at 1967 Calvert St NW, this family-owned restaurant is decorated with a mural featuring Mama Ayesha and every U.S. president since Eisenhower. Website: https://www.mamaayeshas.com/; Average prices: $10-$25.

5. **Florida Avenue Grill:** Established in 1944, Florida Avenue Grill is one of the oldest soul food restaurants in the United States. Located at 1100 Florida Ave NW, the restaurant is known for its mouthwatering Southern classics like fried chicken, collard greens, and sweet potato pie. Website: https://www.floridaavenuegrill.com/; Average prices: $10-$25.
6. **Astro Doughnuts & Fried Chicken:** For a unique D.C. experience, visit Astro Doughnuts & Fried Chicken at 1308 G St NW. This popular spot offers gourmet doughnuts in creative flavors, as well as savory fried chicken sandwiches. Website: https://www.astrodoughnuts.com/; Average prices: $3-$10.
7. **District Taco:** This popular eatery, with multiple locations throughout the city, offers authentic Mexican street food, including tacos, burritos, and quesadillas. Their focus on fresh ingredients and customizable menu options make District Taco a local favorite. Website: https://www.districttaco.com/; Average prices: $8-$15.
8. **&Pizza:** A D.C. original, &Pizza serves up delicious, customizable oblong-shaped pizzas with a variety of toppings and sauces to choose from. With several locations throughout the city, &Pizza is a convenient and satisfying option for a quick meal. Website: https://andpizza.com ; Average prices: $10-$15.
9. **Bluejacket Brewery:** Located in a historic building at 300 Tingey St SE, Bluejacket Brewery offers a rotating selection of craft beers brewed on-site, along with a menu of elevated pub fare. Enjoy your meal in their spacious industrial-chic dining room or on their outdoor patio. Website: https://bluejacketdc.com ; Average prices: $10-$25.
10. **Ethiopic:** Situated at 401 H St NE, Ethiopic offers traditional Ethiopian cuisine in a warm, inviting atmosphere. Share a variety of flavorful dishes, served on a large platter with injera bread, for a communal dining experience. Website: http://www.ethiopicrestaurant.com/; Average prices: $15-$30.

11. **Rasika:** Renowned for its modern Indian cuisine, Rasika has two locations in the city (633 D St NW and 1190 New Hampshire Ave NW). Enjoy their famous palak chaat, tandoori dishes, and an extensive wine list in a stylish, contemporary setting. Website: https://www.rasikarestaurant.com ; Average prices: $20-$40.

These iconic D.C. eateries and food traditions offer a taste of the city's diverse culinary landscape, providing memorable dining experiences for locals and visitors alike. Be sure to check out these establishments during your visit to Washington, D.C. to sample some of the best food the city has to offer.

8.2 International Flavors: D.C.'s Diverse Dining Scene

Washington, D.C.'s diverse dining scene offers a wide range of international flavors, showcasing the city's multicultural heritage. From Ethiopian to Peruvian, here are some of the top restaurants representing the global cuisine found in the nation's capital:

Zenebech Restaurant: This family-owned Ethiopian restaurant, located at 2420 18th St NW, is known for its authentic flavors and generous portions. Enjoy a variety of traditional dishes, like doro wat and tibs, served with injera bread. Website: https://www.zenebechdc.com/; Average prices: $10-$25.

Doi Moi: Situated at 1800 14th St NW, Doi Moi offers Southeast Asian cuisine with a focus on Vietnamese and Thai flavors. Their menu features dishes such as banh xeo, green papaya salad, and various curries. Website: https://www.doimoidc.com/; Average prices: $12-$28.

Oyamel Cocina Mexicana: Part of the renowned José Andrés restaurant group, Oyamel Cocina Mexicana serves contemporary Mexican fare in a vibrant, modern setting at 401 7th St NW. Enjoy their innovative small plates, like the chapulines (grasshoppers) or ceviche. Website: https://www.oyamel.com/; Average prices: $8-$25.

Jaleo: Another gem from José Andrés, Jaleo is a Spanish tapas restaurant with multiple locations in the D.C. area. Indulge in a variety of small plates, like patatas bravas and gambas al ajillo, along with paella and sangria. Website: https://www.jaleo.com/; Average prices: $8-$30.

Little Serow: This intimate eatery at 1511 17th St NW offers a unique dining experience, serving a fixed menu of Northern Thai dishes with bold flavors and family-style service. Reservations are highly recommended due to limited seating. Website: http://www.littleserow.com/; Average prices: $60 per person for a prix-fixe menu.

Le Diplomate: Bringing a taste of Paris to D.C., Le Diplomate is a popular French brasserie located at 1601 14th St NW. Enjoy classic French dishes like steak frites, escargot, and onion soup in a bustling, elegant atmosphere. Website: https://www.lediplomatedc.com/; Average prices: $15-$40.

Pisco y Nazca: This lively Peruvian restaurant, located at 1823 L St NW, offers a modern twist on traditional dishes, such as ceviche, lomo saltado, and causa. Pair your meal with a refreshing pisco sour for the ultimate Peruvian dining experience. Website: https://piscoynazca.com/washington-dc/; Average prices: $12-$28.

Sushi Taro: At 1503 17th St NW, Sushi Taro offers a refined Japanese dining experience, featuring traditional sushi and sashimi, as well as kaiseki (multi-course) meals. The restaurant has been awarded a Michelin star for its exceptional cuisine and service. Website: https://www.sushitaro.com ; Average prices: $20-$100.

The Red Hen: Located at 1822 1st St NW, The Red Hen offers Italian-inspired cuisine with a focus on seasonal, locally sourced ingredients. Enjoy house-made pasta dishes, such as rigatoni with fennel sausage ragu and ricotta cavatelli, in a cozy, rustic atmosphere. Website: https://www.theredhendc.com/; Average prices: $15-$30.

Rasika West End: A sister restaurant to the acclaimed Rasika, Rasika West End is located at 1190 New Hampshire Ave NW and serves modern Indian cuisine. With dishes like crispy spinach palak chaat and black cod in a banana leaf, this elegant eatery is a must-visit for fans of Indian food. Website: https://www.rasikarestaurant.com/westend/; Average prices: $15-$35.

Maketto: A unique combination of a restaurant, café, and retail space, Maketto is located at 1351 H St NE and offers a fusion of Cambodian and Taiwanese cuisine. Savor dishes like Taiwanese fried chicken or num pang sandwiches in a stylish, communal setting. Website: https://maketto1351.com/; Average prices: $8-$25.

Ambar: Situated at 523 8th St SE, Ambar brings the flavors of the Balkans to the heart of Washington, D.C. Enjoy a variety of small plates, like stuffed sour cabbage and grilled meats, as well as rakia, a traditional fruit brandy. Website: https://www.ambarrestaurant.com/; Average prices: $6-$15.

These are just a few of the international flavors that can be found in Washington, D.C. Be sure to explore the city's diverse dining scene to discover even more unique culinary experiences from around the globe.

8.3 Farm-to-Table and Sustainable Dining

Washington, D.C. is home to a growing number of restaurants that prioritize farm-to-table and sustainable dining practices, showcasing the city's commitment to supporting local farmers and promoting eco-friendly initiatives. These eateries offer fresh, seasonal ingredients, often sourced from nearby farms, and focus on sustainable practices in their operations. Below are some of the top farm-to-table and sustainable dining options in the nation's capital:

Farmers Fishers Bakers: Located at 3000 K St NW, this waterfront restaurant is owned by a collective of American family farmers and features a diverse menu with ingredients sourced from their farms. Enjoy dishes like brick-oven pizza, sushi, and freshly baked bread. Website: https://www.farmersfishersbakers.com/; Average prices: $12-$30.

Founding Farmers: With multiple locations in the D.C. area, Founding Farmers is another restaurant owned by the same collective behind Farmers Fishers Bakers. They offer a menu of farm-to-table American classics, such as pot roast, fried chicken, and house-made pastas. Website: https://www.wearefoundingfarmers.com/; Average prices: $12-$30.

Blue Duck Tavern: Situated at 1201 24th St NW, Blue Duck Tavern is a Michelin-starred restaurant that prides itself on its farm-to-table ethos. The seasonal menu highlights the finest ingredients from regional farms and features dishes like wood-oven roasted bone marrow and slow-cooked short ribs. Website: https://www.blueducktavern.com/; Average prices: $20-$50.

Equinox: Located at 818 Connecticut Ave NW, Equinox offers a menu that combines the flavors of the Mid-Atlantic with sustainable, locally sourced ingredients. Chef Todd Gray's innovative dishes, like Maryland crab cakes and vegan pasta, cater to both carnivores and vegetarians. Website: https://www.equinoxrestaurant.com/; Average prices: $15-$40.

The Dabney: Situated in D.C.'s Shaw neighborhood at 122 Blagden Alley NW, The Dabney sources ingredients from Mid-Atlantic farms and purveyors, crafting a menu that pays homage to the region's culinary heritage. The open kitchen features a wood-burning hearth, adding a rustic touch to dishes like ember-roasted carrots and wood-grilled pork chops. Website: https://www.thedabney.com/; Average prices: $12-$38.

Iron Gate: Located at 1734 N St NW, Iron Gate offers Mediterranean-inspired cuisine in a romantic setting, with a focus on sustainable, locally sourced ingredients. Enjoy dishes like wood-grilled octopus and ricotta gnocchi in their idyllic courtyard or historic dining room. Website: https://www.irongaterestaurantdc.com/; Average prices: $15-$35.

Sustainable dining extends beyond farm-to-table practices, with some restaurants also emphasizing eco-friendly design, energy efficiency, and waste reduction. When dining in Washington, D.C., look for establishments that prioritize sustainability, supporting the city's commitment to a greener, more conscious dining experience.

8.4 Craft Breweries, Wineries, and Distilleries

Washington, D.C.'s thriving craft beverage scene offers a wide variety of local breweries, wineries, and distilleries, each with their unique take on classic libations and innovative new creations. Whether you're a fan of hoppy IPAs, bold red wines, or handcrafted spirits, the nation's capital has something to suit your palate. Here are some must-visit craft breweries, wineries, and distilleries in and around Washington, D.C.:

Craft Breweries

DC Brau: As the first production brewery to open within D.C. city limits since the 1950s, DC Brau has been a pioneer in the local craft beer scene. Their brewery and taproom, located at 3178-B Bladensburg Rd NE, offers a wide range of brews, including their flagship IPA, The Corruption. Website: https://dcbrau.com/; Average prices: $6-$12.

Right Proper Brewing Company: With two locations in the D.C. area, Right Proper Brewing Company focuses on creating flavorful, unique beers that showcase a variety of styles. Visit their brewpub at 624 T St NW or their production house and tasting room at 920 Girard St NE. Website: https://www.rightproperbrewing.com/; Average prices: $5-$10.

Bluejacket: Located at 300 Tingey St SE, Bluejacket is a brewery, restaurant, and bar housed in a century-old former ship and munitions manufacturing facility. They offer an extensive lineup of beers, with more than 20 options on tap, ranging from classic styles to experimental brews. Website: https://www.bluejacketdc.com/; Average prices: $6-$12.

Wineries

District Winery: As D.C.'s first urban winery, District Winery sources grapes from across the country to create small-batch, premium wines. Located at 385 Water St SE, the winery offers wine tastings, a full-service restaurant, and beautiful waterfront views. Website: https://districtwinery.com/; Average prices: $10-$20 for wine tastings.

City Winery: This unique concept, located at 1350 Okie St NE, combines a winery, restaurant, and concert venue, offering a one-of-a-kind experience for wine and music enthusiasts. Enjoy a selection of house-made wines, along with a diverse lineup of live music performances. Website: https://citywinery.com/washingtondc/; Average prices: $10-$20 for wine tastings.

Distilleries

District Distilling Co.: Situated at 1414 U St NW, District Distilling Co. is a combination distillery, restaurant, and bar. Their line of spirits includes gin, whiskey, rum, and vodka, all crafted on-site. Stop by for a distillery tour and enjoy craft cocktails featuring their artisanal spirits. Website: https://www.district-distilling.com/; Average prices: $10-$15 for cocktails.

One Eight Distilling: Named after Article One, Section Eight of the U.S. Constitution, One Eight Distilling is dedicated to producing finely crafted spirits in the nation's capital. Located at 1135 Okie St NE, their offerings include whiskey, gin, and vodka, all distilled from locally sourced ingredients. Visit their tasting room to sample their creations and learn more about the distilling process. Website: https://www.oneeightdistilling.com/; Average prices: $10-$15 for cocktails.

Republic Restoratives: As a women-owned, small-batch distillery and cocktail bar, Republic Restoratives is committed to producing high-quality spirits with a focus on craftsmanship and sustainability. Located at 1369 New York Ave NE, their lineup includes vodka, bourbon, and rye whiskey. Stop by their Ivy Room cocktail bar for expertly crafted cocktails and a relaxed atmosphere. Website: https://republicrestoratives.com/; Average prices: $10-$15 for cocktails.

With so many options for craft beverages in Washington, D.C., you'll find plenty of opportunities to explore the local scene and discover your new favorite beer, wine, or spirit.

8.5 Our Top Five Dining Spots in Washington, D.C.

We're excited to share with you our top five favorite dining places in the city, offering a range of delicious and satisfying options:

1. **Chopt (1629 K Street):** Kicking off our list with a healthy choice, Chopt is a salad-centric restaurant that takes pride in using a wide variety of fresh ingredients. While they offer a pre-set salad menu, you can also customize your own creation from an extensive selection of ingredients. These generously-sized salads typically cost around $10 per person, including drinks. Enjoy a wholesome, delicious meal at this popular spot.

2. **Ben's Chili Bowl** (1213 U Street): A quintessential American eatery, Ben's Chili Bowl specializes in hot dogs and burgers. This iconic spot gained even more fame when President Obama dined here just one day after being elected. While not recommended for those

sensitive to spice, as many of their sauces pack a punch, this historic Washington, D.C. establishment offers a satisfying meal for under $10.

3. **&Pizza (1118 H Street):** Often regarded as the best pizza in town, &Pizza boasts a wide selection of delicious pies, including a scrumptious chocolate-covered dessert pizza. The only drawback is the limited seating in this small, typically bustling establishment. To enjoy a more leisurely dining experience, consider visiting during off-peak hours.

4. **Dupont Italian Kitchen** (*1637 17th Street*): Italian eateries are consistently a reliable choice for enjoyable dining experiences worldwide. This specific Italian restaurant offers high-quality meals at very reasonable prices. Additionally, it features a terrace for al fresco dining during the warmer months. While it may be a simple and traditional Italian restaurant, it is undoubtedly a fantastic option for savoring delicious food at an affordable price in Washington, D.C.

5. **Sushi Taro** (*1503 17th Street*): The area surrounding this Japanese restaurant is relatively quiet until you reach the bustling intersection of 17th Street and P Street. Here, you'll find lively bar terraces and young patrons enjoying food and drinks. Sushi Taro is situated on the first floor, and by 8 PM, a line typically forms outside its entrance. The restaurant features several distinct dining areas: a main room with traditional tables, a bar that spans the length of the kitchen, a section for floor seating, and a separate exclusive room. While Sushi Taro's prices are significantly higher than the other options we've mentioned in this section, it's worth considering if

you're a fan of Japanese cuisine, as it is widely regarded as the best sushi spot in the entire city.

8.6 Best Burger Spots in Washington DC

Washington DC takes pride in providing some of the best burgers in the country. Since Washington is the capital of the state, and United States is the perfect country when it comes to burgers, it makes total sense. Here we'll give you a list of where to find the best burgers in town.

#1: Duke's Grocery – 1513 17th Street

Let's start with the most important: these burgers have twice the amount of meat than regular burgers. With onion, garlic aleoli and Gouda cheese, *The Proper Burger* is delicious. Another highlight is that here the burgers are prepared using a sweet and spicy sauce.

#2: Good Stuff Eatery – 303 Pennsylvania Avenue

Instead of traditional steak burgers, at this place we recommend you try the excellent champignon burger, a portobello mushroom filled with two kinds of cheese. This burger is original and worth the price.

#3: Eatonville– 2121 14th Street

Following the pattern of trying something different than steak burgers, at Eatonville, we recommend the beans burger. You won't regret it, it's ridiculously good.

#4: Le Diplomat – 1601 14th Street

Le Diplomat's burgers are considered to be the best in Washington DC by the prestigious Zagat guide, and we agree. Just try these burgers and see it (or taste it) by yourself.

9. Family-Friendly Attractions and Activities

Washington, D.C. offers a plethora of family-friendly attractions and activities, making it an ideal destination for a fun-filled vacation with your loved ones. From interactive museums to engaging outdoor spaces, the city has something to entertain and educate visitors of all ages.

9.1 Educational Adventures for Kids

In this section, we will explore some of the top educational adventures for kids in the nation's capital.

1. **National Museum of Natural History:** This popular museum, located at 10th St. & Constitution Ave. NW, is a must-visit destination for families. With exhibits on dinosaurs, ocean life, and mammals, the museum provides an engaging and educational experience for children and adults alike. Don't miss the Hope

Diamond and the Butterfly Pavilion. Website:
https://naturalhistory.si.edu/

2. **National Air and Space Museum:** Featuring a vast collection of
    aircraft and spacecraft, this museum at Independence Ave. & 6th St.
    SW sparks the imagination of kids and adults alike. Explore the
    history of aviation, learn about the solar system, and even try your
    hand at piloting a simulated aircraft. Website:
    https://airandspace.si.edu/

3. **Smithsonian National Zoo:** Home to more than 2,700 animals
    representing 390 species, the National Zoo at 3001 Connecticut Ave.
    NW offers a fun and educational experience for the whole family.
    Highlights include the Giant Panda Habitat, Elephant Trails, and the
    Kid's Farm. Admission is free. Website: https://nationalzoo.si.edu/

4. **The International Spy Museum: This** interactive museum at 700
    L'Enfant Plaza SW offers a fascinating and engaging look into the
    world of espionage. Kids can participate in hands-on exhibits, learn
    about famous spies, and even take on their own spy missions.
    Website: https://www.spymuseum.org/

5. **The National Building Museum:** Located at 401 F St. NW, this
    museum is dedicated to the history and impact of architecture and
    design. With interactive exhibits and hands-on activities, kids can
    learn about the built environment while having fun. Don't miss the
    Building Zone, a space designed specifically for young children to
    explore and create. Website: https://www.nbm.org/

These are just a few of the many educational adventures awaiting kids
and families in Washington, D.C. With so much to see and do, you'll
never run out of fun and engaging activities to enjoy together.

9.2 Fun and Games: Playgrounds, Amusement Centers, and Arcades

Washington, D.C. offers a variety of fun and engaging activities for families to enjoy, from playgrounds and amusement centers to arcades. These entertainment options provide a chance for kids to expend energy, socialize, and create lasting memories. Here are some top picks for fun and games in the nation's capital:

1. **Clemyjontri Park:** Located at 6317 Georgetown Pike in McLean, VA, just outside of D.C., Clemyjontri Park is a colorful, inclusive playground designed for children of all abilities. The park features wheelchair-accessible equipment, swings, slides, and various interactive play structures. Website: https://www.fairfaxcounty.gov/parks/clemyjontri

2. **National Gallery of Art Sculpture Garden:** Situated at 7th St. & Constitution Ave. NW, this outdoor space offers a unique blend of art and play. Kids can explore the various sculptures, while adults can relax and enjoy the surroundings. In the winter, the garden's central fountain transforms into an ice-skating rink. Website: https://www.nga.gov/visit/sculpture-garden.html

3. **Smithsonian Carousel:** Located on the National Mall between the Smithsonian Castle and the National Museum of American History, this historic carousel offers a delightful ride for children and adults alike. Enjoy the charming scenery as you whirl around on one of the beautifully carved horses. Website: https://www.si.edu/carousel

4. **Dave & Buster's:** This family-friendly entertainment center at 6655 Springfield Mall, Springfield, VA, offers a wide variety of arcade games, virtual reality experiences, and more. Enjoy classic games like skee-ball and air hockey or try your hand at the latest video games. The venue also features a restaurant and bar. Website: https://www.daveandbusters.com/locations/springfield

5. **Ultrazone Laser Tag:** Located at 3447 Carlin Springs Rd, Falls Church, VA, Ultrazone Laser Tag is an exciting destination for family fun. Battle it out in the multi-level laser tag arena, strategize with your team, and enjoy the thrill of competition. Website: https://www.ultralasertag.com/
6. **Escape Room Live:** With multiple locations in the D.C. area, including 3345 M St NW, Escape Room Live offers a unique, interactive experience for the whole family. Work together to solve puzzles and clues in order to escape a themed room within a set time limit. Website: https://www.escaperoomlive.com/

These are just a sampling of the numerous fun and game options available to families in and around Washington, D.C. Whether you're seeking outdoor adventure, indoor excitement, or a combination of both, you'll find plenty of ways to bond and create lasting memories together.

9.3 Family-Friendly Dining Options

Washington, D.C. offers a variety of family-friendly dining options that cater to the needs and tastes of both children and adults. These establishments provide kid-approved menus, comfortable atmospheres, and a welcoming environment for the whole family. Here are some top picks for family-friendly dining in the nation's capital:

1. **Ted's Bulletin:** With multiple locations in the D.C. area, including 1818 14th St NW, Ted's Bulletin is a nostalgic diner known for its comfort food and homemade pop tarts. The menu features a wide selection of classic American dishes, as well as a dedicated kids' menu. Website: https://www.tedsbulletin.com/
2. **Busboys and Poets:** A unique combination of restaurant, bookstore, and community gathering space, Busboys and Poets

offers a diverse menu with options for everyone in the family. The kid's menu includes favorites like grilled cheese, pasta, and quesadillas. Multiple locations are available, including 2021 14th St NW. Website: https://www.busboysandpoets.com/

3. **Matchbox:** This family-friendly pizzeria offers a variety of delicious wood-fired pizzas, as well as other American classics. With a dedicated kids' menu and a lively atmosphere, Matchbox is a great choice for a meal out with the whole family. Locations include 1901 14th St NW. Website: https://www.matchboxrestaurants.com/

4. **Silver Diner:** With a retro diner atmosphere and a focus on local, fresh ingredients, Silver Diner is a popular choice for families. The menu includes classic diner fare as well as healthier options, with a separate kids' menu featuring organic and gluten-free choices. Locations in the D.C. area include 3200 Wilson Blvd, Arlington, VA. Website: https://www.silverdiner.com/

5. **Oyamel Cocina Mexicana:** Located at 401 7th St NW, this José Andrés restaurant offers a modern twist on Mexican cuisine in a colorful, family-friendly setting. The menu features a variety of small plates, including kid-friendly options like tacos and quesadillas. Website: https://www.oyamel.com/

6. **Founding Farmers**: This farm-to-table restaurant, located at 1924 Pennsylvania Ave NW, offers a wide range of American dishes made with fresh, locally sourced ingredients. The kid's menu features wholesome options like grilled chicken, pasta, and mini cheeseburgers. Website: https://www.wearefoundingfarmers.com/

7. **Comet Ping Pong:** This fun and casual pizzeria, located at 5037 Connecticut Ave NW, features tasty wood-fired pizzas and an on-site ping pong table for added entertainment. The laid-back atmosphere and engaging activities make it an ideal spot for a family meal. Website: https://www.cometpingpong.com/

These family-friendly dining options in Washington, D.C. provide a variety of cuisine choices and welcoming environments to ensure a memorable dining experience for the entire family.

9.4 Tips for Traveling with Kids in D.C.

Washington, D.C., offers a wealth of attractions and activities for families, but traveling with children can present its own set of challenges. Here are some helpful tips to make your family trip to the nation's capital more enjoyable and stress-free:

1. Plan ahead: Research and create an itinerary that includes kid-friendly attractions, restaurants, and accommodations. Keep in mind the interests and energy levels of your children when planning your days.
2. Prioritize attractions: D.C. has numerous museums, monuments, and historical sites to visit. Select the most important ones for your family and allocate enough time for each. Be flexible and adjust your schedule as needed.
3. Utilize public transportation: The Washington Metropolitan Area Transit Authority (WMATA) operates the Metrorail and Metrobus systems, providing convenient and affordable options for getting around the city. Consider purchasing a SmarTrip card for easy access to public transportation.
4. Bring a stroller or carrier: For younger children, a stroller or baby carrier can make navigating the city easier and provide a place for them to rest during long days of sightseeing.
5. Pack snacks and water: Keep your kids hydrated and energized with healthy snacks and water throughout the day. This will help prevent meltdowns and keep everyone in good spirits.

6. Schedule downtime: Plan for breaks and downtime in your itinerary to prevent overstimulation and exhaustion. This may include returning to your hotel for a nap or finding a park to relax in.

7. Take advantage of free attractions: Many of D.C.'s top attractions, such as the Smithsonian museums, the National Gallery of Art, and the National Zoo, offer free admission. Make the most of these free attractions to entertain your family without breaking the bank.

8. Dress for the weather: Washington, D.C., can experience varying weather conditions throughout the year. Check the forecast before your trip and pack appropriate clothing, such as rain gear or sunscreen, to ensure your family's comfort.

9. Book family-friendly accommodations: Consider booking a hotel or vacation rental that offers family-friendly amenities like a pool, playground, or game room. This will help keep your kids entertained during downtime and make your stay more comfortable.

10. Keep safety in mind: Make sure your kids know your contact information and have a plan in case you get separated. Consider using a buddy system or child locator devices for added security.

By following these tips, you can help ensure a fun, memorable, and stress-free family trip to Washington, D.C.

10. Beyond the Capital: Day Trips and Excursions

10.1 Historical Sites and Battlefields

Venturing beyond Washington, D.C., offers numerous opportunities to explore historical sites, battlefields, and landmarks that played significant roles in American history. Here are a few day trip ideas to immerse yourself in the rich history that surrounds the nation's capital:

1. **Gettysburg National Military Park, Pennsylvania:** Just a 90-minute drive from D.C., Gettysburg National Military Park is the site of the famous Battle of Gettysburg, a turning point in the American Civil War. Visitors can take guided tours of the battlefield, visit the Gettysburg Museum and Visitor Center, and explore the Soldiers' National Cemetery. Website: https://www.nps.gov/gett/index.htm

2. **Harpers Ferry National Historical Park, West Virginia:** Located about an hour's drive from Washington, D.C., Harpers Ferry offers a mix of history and natural beauty. Explore the picturesque town, visit the site of John Brown's Raid, and enjoy scenic hiking trails along the Potomac and Shenandoah Rivers. Website: https://www.nps.gov/hafe/index.htm

3. **Mount Vernon, Virginia:** Just a 30-minute drive from D.C., George Washington's Mount Vernon estate offers an in-depth look at the life of America's first president. Tour the mansion, stroll through the beautiful gardens, and visit the museum to learn more about George Washington's life and legacy. Website: https://www.mountvernon.org/

4. **Antietam National Battlefield, Maryland:** A little over an hour's drive from the capital, Antietam National Battlefield is the site of the bloodiest single-day battle in American history. Take a self-guided tour of the battlefield, visit the visitor center, and pay your respects at the Antietam National Cemetery. Website: https://www.nps.gov/anti/index.htm

5. **Monticello, Virginia:** Just over two hours from Washington, D.C., Monticello, the home of Thomas Jefferson, offers a fascinating look at the life and times of the third U.S. president. Explore the mansion, grounds, and gardens, and visit the on-site museum to learn more about Jefferson's many accomplishments. Website: https://www.monticello.org/

These historical sites and battlefields provide excellent day trip opportunities for history buffs and families looking to delve deeper into America's past. Make sure to check each site's website for hours, admission fees, and special events before planning your visit.

10.2 Charming Small Towns and Villages

The area surrounding Washington, D.C., is rich with charming small towns and villages that offer unique experiences, local shops, and a sense of stepping back in time. Here are some picturesque towns you should consider visiting on a day trip from the nation's capital:

1. Annapolis, Maryland: Just a 45-minute drive from D.C., Annapolis is a historic waterfront town and the capital of Maryland. Stroll through the charming downtown area, visit the United States Naval Academy, and enjoy a meal at one of the many waterside restaurants. Website: https://www.visitannapolis.org/

2. Leesburg, Virginia: Located about an hour's drive from Washington, D.C., Leesburg is a quaint town with a rich history. Explore the historic downtown district, shop at local boutiques, and visit nearby wineries and breweries. Website: https://www.visitloudoun.org/towns-and-areas/leesburg/

3. Frederick, Maryland: Just over an hour from D.C., Frederick boasts a lively arts and culture scene, historic architecture, and unique shopping and dining options. Visit the National Museum of Civil War Medicine, or explore the city's many art galleries and antique shops. Website: https://www.visitfrederick.org/

4. Middleburg, Virginia: Nestled in the heart of Virginia's horse and wine country, Middleburg is a picturesque small town with a charming main street lined with boutiques, galleries, and restaurants. Enjoy wine tastings at nearby wineries, or take a scenic drive

through the rolling countryside. Website:
https://www.visitloudoun.org/towns-and-areas/middleburg/

5. St. Michaels, Maryland: Situated on the Chesapeake Bay, St. Michaels is a historic waterfront town known for its maritime heritage. Explore the Chesapeake Bay Maritime Museum, take a cruise on the bay, or relax at a waterfront restaurant while enjoying fresh seafood. Website: https://www.stmichaelsmd.org/

These charming small towns and villages provide a perfect escape from the hustle and bustle of Washington, D.C. Whether you're seeking history, culture, or natural beauty, each town offers a unique experience just a short drive from the capital.

10.3 Natural Wonders and Scenic Drives

While Washington, D.C. is known for its bustling city life, the surrounding areas are home to stunning natural wonders and scenic drives that are worth exploring. Here are some of the top natural attractions and drives to consider for a day trip or weekend getaway:

Shenandoah National Park: Located about two hours southwest of Washington, D.C., Shenandoah National Park offers over 500 miles of hiking trails, scenic drives, and panoramic views of the Blue Ridge Mountains. Visitors can also enjoy camping, fishing, and wildlife viewing in the park. Website: https://www.nps.gov/shen/index.htm

Great Falls Park: Just a short drive from the city, Great Falls Park offers stunning views of the Potomac River as it cascades over jagged rocks and falls 76 feet in just a half-mile stretch. Visitors can hike, fish, or take a scenic drive along the park's roads. Website: https://www.nps.gov/grfa/index.htm

Skyline Drive: Located in Shenandoah National Park, Skyline Drive is a 105-mile scenic drive that runs along the crest of the Blue Ridge Mountains. Visitors can take in panoramic views of the surrounding valleys, forests, and peaks, and stop at various overlooks and picnic areas along the way. Website: https://www.nps.gov/shen/planyourvisit/skyline-drive.htm

Catoctin Mountain Park: This park, located in Maryland about an hour from D.C., is home to stunning waterfalls, hiking trails, and historic sites. Visitors can explore the remains of an old iron furnace or hike to the Cunningham Falls, the largest cascading waterfall in Maryland. Website: https://www.nps.gov/cato/index.htm

Chesapeake Bay Beaches: Just a short drive from the city, the beaches of the Chesapeake Bay offer a variety of recreational activities, including swimming, boating, and fishing. Popular beaches include Sandy Point State Park and North Beach. Website: https://www.visitmaryland.org/article/chesapeake-bay-beaches

Whether you're looking for a scenic drive or a chance to explore the great outdoors, these natural wonders near Washington, D.C. are sure to impress.

10.4 Themed Itineraries for Different Interests

If you're looking to plan a day trip or excursion outside of D.C., there are plenty of themed itineraries to suit a variety of interests. Here are some ideas to inspire your next adventure:

Wine and Culinary Tour: Take a scenic drive out to Virginia wine country and sample some of the region's best wines, paired with farm-to-table cuisine. Some top wineries to visit include Barboursville Vineyards, Early Mountain Vineyards, and King Family Vineyards. You can also stop by local farmers' markets and artisanal shops for locally sourced treats along the way.

Outdoor Adventure: For those who love the great outdoors, head out to Shenandoah National Park for a day of hiking, camping, and scenic drives. The park offers over 500 miles of hiking trails, as well as breathtaking views of the Blue Ridge Mountains. If you're feeling adventurous, you can even go rock climbing or white-water rafting in the nearby rivers.

Historic Tour: There are plenty of historic sites and landmarks just a short drive from D.C. For a unique experience, visit Mount Vernon, the historic home of George Washington, or Monticello, the former home of Thomas Jefferson. You can also explore the historic towns of Alexandria, VA or Annapolis, MD, both of which offer plenty of colonial charm.

Art and Culture: Take a day trip to Baltimore, MD and explore the city's vibrant arts and culture scene. Visit the Baltimore Museum of Art, the Walters Art Museum, or the American Visionary Art Museum for a glimpse of the city's diverse artistic offerings. You can also stroll through the city's historic neighborhoods, like Fells Point and Canton, which offer plenty of shops, galleries, and restaurants.

Family Fun: For a day of family-friendly fun, head out to Hershey, PA and explore Hersheypark, a theme park with over 70 rides and attractions. You can also visit Hershey's Chocolate World, where you can take a tour of the chocolate factory and create your own candy bars. For animal lovers, the nearby ZooAmerica offers a chance to see over 200 animals from across North America.

11. Accommodation and Travel Resources

11.1 Choosing the Right Accommodation

Choosing the right accommodation is an important part of any trip, and Washington, D.C. has plenty of options to suit all budgets and preferences. Here are some factors to consider when selecting your accommodation:

1. Location: Consider where you want to be in the city and what is most convenient for your activities. If you want to be in the heart of the city, look for accommodations in the downtown area. If you prefer a more residential vibe, consider staying in one of the neighborhoods outside of the city center.

2. Budget: Determine how much you want to spend on accommodation and narrow down your options accordingly. Keep in mind that prices can vary depending on the time of year and availability, so it's always a good idea to compare prices and book in advance.

3. Amenities: Think about what amenities are important to you, such as free Wi-Fi, breakfast, parking, or a fitness center. Look for accommodations that offer the amenities that are most important to you.

4. Type of Accommodation: There are many different types of accommodation in Washington, D.C., including hotels, motels, hostels, and vacation rentals. Consider what type of accommodation suits your needs and preferences.

5. Reviews: Read reviews from previous guests to get a better understanding of their experiences and any potential issues or concerns with the accommodation.

Once you have considered these factors, you can start looking for the right accommodation for your trip. It's always a good idea to compare prices and book in advance to secure your preferred accommodations.

11.2 Budget and Luxury Hotel Recommendations

Here are some budget and luxury hotel recommendations for travelers visiting Washington, D.C.:

Budget Hotel Recommendations:

1. **HI Washington DC Hostel:** This centrally located hostel offers both private and shared dormitory-style rooms at affordable prices. Guests can enjoy free Wi-Fi, daily breakfast, and a range of social events and activities. Located at 1009 11th St NW. Website: https://www.hiusa.org/hostels/district-of-columbia/washington-dc/washington-dc; Average prices: Dormitory-style rooms from $34 per night, private rooms from $108 per night.
2. **Pod DC Hotel:** This modern micro-hotel offers compact yet stylish rooms at a budget-friendly price. Guests can enjoy free Wi-Fi, a communal lounge area, and an on-site restaurant and bar. Located at 627 H St NW. Website: https://www.podhoteldc.com/; Average prices: Standard rooms from $79 per night, queen rooms from $99 per night.
3. **The LINE Hotel DC:** This trendy hotel offers affordable rooms with a chic, artsy vibe. Located in the heart of Adams Morgan, the hotel features on-site dining, a fitness center, and a coffee shop. Located at 1770 Euclid St NW. Website: https://www.thelinehotel.com/dc/; Average prices: Standard rooms from $115 per night.

Luxury Hotel Recommendations:

1. **The Jefferson, Washington, DC: This** luxurious boutique hotel offers elegantly appointed rooms and suites, featuring classic decor and modern amenities. The hotel boasts multiple dining options, a fitness center, and a spa. Located at 1200 16th St NW. Website: https://www.jeffersondc.com/; Average prices: Deluxe rooms from $400 per night, suites from $650 per night.
2. **The Watergate Hotel:** This iconic hotel offers a sophisticated blend of mid-century modern design and contemporary luxury. The hotel features an on-site restaurant, a rooftop bar and lounge, a spa, and a fitness center. Located at 2650 Virginia Ave NW. Website: https://www.thewatergatehotel.com/; Average prices: Deluxe rooms from $350 per night, suites from $700 per night.
3. **The Hay-Adams:** This historic hotel offers luxurious accommodations with stunning views of the White House and Lafayette Square. The hotel features on-site dining, a fitness center, and a rooftop terrace. Located at 800 16th St NW. Website: https://www.hayadams.com/; Average prices: Deluxe rooms from $500 per night, suites from $800 per night.

11.3 Hostels, Bed & Breakfasts, and Vacation Rentals

For travelers on a budget or those looking for a more unique travel experience, Washington, D.C. offers a variety of alternative accommodation options, including hostels, bed & breakfasts, and vacation rentals. Here are some recommendations:

Hostels:

- **HI Washington DC Hostel:** Located in the heart of downtown D.C. at 1009 11th St NW, this hostel offers dorm-style and private rooms at affordable prices. It also has a communal kitchen, free breakfast, and a variety of social activities for guests. Website: https://www.hiusa.org/hostels/district-of-columbia/washington-dc/dc; Average prices: $25-$80 per person per night.

- **Duo Housing Hostel:** This trendy hostel at 1223 11th St NW offers a mix of private and shared rooms, as well as a communal kitchen and lounge. It's located in the trendy Logan Circle neighborhood, with plenty of bars and restaurants nearby. Website: https://duohousing.com/dc-hostel/; Average prices: $30-$80 per person per night.

Bed & Breakfasts:

- **Akwaaba DC:** This beautiful bed & breakfast at 1708 16th St NW is housed in a historic mansion and features elegant rooms, a delicious breakfast, and a relaxing courtyard. It's located in the trendy Dupont Circle neighborhood, with plenty of dining and shopping options nearby. Website: https://www.akwaabadc.com/; Average prices: $150-$300 per night.
- **American Guest House:** Situated in a historic townhouse at 2005 Columbia Rd NW, this cozy bed & breakfast offers comfortable rooms, a daily breakfast buffet, and a convenient location near the Adams Morgan neighborhood. Website: https://www.americanguesthouse.com/; Average prices: $125-$250 per night.

Vacation Rentals:

- Airbnb: As in most cities, Airbnb has a wide variety of vacation rentals available in Washington, D.C., ranging from private rooms to entire apartments or houses. Prices vary depending on the location and amenities. Website: https://www.airbnb.com/; Average prices: $50-$300 per night.
- Vrbo: Similar to Airbnb, Vrbo also offers a variety of vacation rentals in D.C., including apartments, townhouses, and houses.

Many rentals are located in historic neighborhoods, giving visitors a chance to experience life like a local. Website: https://www.vrbo.com/; Average prices: $50-$500 per night.

11.4 Essential Travel Tips and Safety Advice

When planning a trip to Washington, D.C., it's important to keep in mind some essential travel tips and safety advice to ensure a smooth and enjoyable experience. Here are some tips to keep in mind:

- Be prepared for security measures: As the capital of the United States, Washington, D.C. has a significant presence of security measures, particularly around government buildings and monuments. Be prepared to go through metal detectors and bag checks, and avoid bringing items that could be considered dangerous or suspicious.

- Use public transportation: D.C.'s public transportation system, including the Metro subway and bus system, is an efficient and affordable way to get around the city. Consider purchasing a SmarTrip card to make using public transportation easier.

- Dress appropriately: Depending on the season, the weather in D.C. can vary widely. Be sure to check the forecast and dress accordingly, particularly if you plan on spending time outside visiting monuments and landmarks.

- Stay aware of your surroundings: As with any major city, it's important to stay aware of your surroundings and be cautious of any suspicious activity. Stick to well-lit and populated areas, particularly at night, and avoid carrying large amounts of cash or valuables.

- Stay hydrated: D.C. can get hot and humid during the summer months, so it's important to stay hydrated. Be sure to carry a water bottle with you and take advantage of the many public water fountains throughout the city.

- Plan ahead for popular attractions: Many of D.C.'s most popular attractions, such as the Smithsonian museums and the National Mall, can get crowded, particularly during peak travel times. Consider booking tickets or making reservations in advance to avoid long lines and wait times.

- Be respectful of cultural and historical sites: D.C. is home to many important cultural and historical sites, so be sure to treat them with respect. Follow posted rules and regulations, avoid touching or climbing on monuments and statues, and be mindful of noise levels and other visitors.

- To fully appreciate Washington DC, it is recommended to avoid rushing your itinerary and try to see everything on the first day of your stay. Despite being a popular destination, the city is not overwhelmingly large. Take your time to enjoy the different attractions it has to offer and distribute them evenly over the course of your three-day visit.

- Consider visiting Washington DC during the **Cherry Blossom National Festival** in April. The city's 3,700 cherry trees, gifted by Japan in the early 20th century, bloom during this time, creating a stunning display of natural beauty. Additionally, the weather during this season is typically perfect for exploring the city.

- Take advantage of the **free monuments and museums**. One of the best things about Washington DC is that many of the city's most iconic attractions are free to visit, making it a great option for budget-conscious travelers.

- Consider **Airbnb** as an alternative to expensive hotels. With hotels in the city often being pricey, Airbnb can be a cost-effective option for finding comfortable and affordable accommodation. There are plenty of listings throughout the city, providing a range of options to suit different preferences and budgets.

- Use credit cards instead of cash. Credit cards are widely accepted throughout the city, making it easy to make purchases without carrying around large amounts of cash. This can help ensure your safety while also providing a convenient way to manage your expenses.

- Take advantage of happy hour deals. Many pubs and restaurants in the city offer discounted food and drinks during happy hour, typically between 4 and 7 PM. Planning your meals around these deals can help you save money while still enjoying delicious cuisine and beverages. Consider having a mid-morning brunch and then dinner around 6:30 to make the most of the happy hour discounts and save between $15 to $20 per person each day.

12.Our Detailed 3-Day Travel Itinerary

1st Day In Washington DC - Itinerary

9:00

Arrival at Dulles Airport (IAD) or Ronald Reagan Airport (DCA)

9:30

When arriving in Washington DC, it is recommended to use the metro or bus to get to your hotel or Airbnb apartment. The city has a well-connected transportation system that is efficient and affordable. The Metro is the most convenient way to travel around the city, and there are various options available depending on your budget and schedule. The cost of a one-way metro ticket varies between $2.00 and $6.00, depending on the distance traveled and the time of day.

If you're planning to stay in the Downtown or East End areas, you will be within walking distance of most of the city's attractions, making it convenient to explore the area on foot. However, if you prefer to stay in a more budget-friendly location or somewhere further away from the center, there are plenty of affordable accommodation options available throughout the city that are well-connected by the metro.

It is also worth noting that the city's transportation system is accessible for those with disabilities, and there are various resources available to ensure a smooth and comfortable travel experience for all visitors. Overall, it is recommended to plan your transportation and accommodation in advance to make the most out of your trip to Washington DC.

10:15

Upon your arrival at the hotel or apartment, take some time to check-in and settle down after your flight before embarking on your 3-day journey exploring Washington DC. Resting for a while will help you to recharge your batteries and be ready to fully enjoy all the exciting activities and attractions that the city has to offer.

11:00 - Head to the White House.

Starting your exploration of the capital of the United States by admiring its most iconic building is a great idea. Although visiting the inside of the White House is almost impossible, as you need to submit a request three months in advance and even then it is very difficult to obtain permission, simply taking a good look at it from the outside is well worth it and a great way to begin your Washington DC experience. For more information about the White House, please refer to ZoomTip 1.1.

12:30

We recommend starting your Washington DC exploration by visiting its most iconic building, the White House, which you can admire from the outside as the submission process to visit inside can be challenging. Afterward, head to a nearby grocery store to buy some food for a picnic and make your way to the National Mall, a vast park dotted with several monuments and free museums. We suggest not trying to see everything in one day.

On your first day, take a leisurely stroll around the park from the Lincoln Memorial to the United States Capitol and look for a good spot to relax and enjoy your picnic. Don't miss visiting the National Museum of American History, the National Museum of Natural History, the National Gallery of Art Sculpture Garden, and the National Gallery of Art, the latter being easily among the best museums in the world in terms of artwork quantity, variety, and quality. The National Museum of Natural History is also a must-visit and considered one of the best of its kind.

By exploring the park and visiting these four museums, you'll have plenty to keep you entertained for the entire day. You can save some of the other incredible museums for another day. For more details about the National Mall and its museums and monuments, check out ZoomTip 1.2.

18:00

Head back to the hotel/apartment and get some rest before dinner.

19:00

Enjoy a delightful dinner at one of the recommended dining places in Washington DC that we have listed in the "Our Favorite Dining Places in Washington DC" section. You will find a diverse range of options based on the type of cuisine you prefer.

21:30

Experience a live jazz performance at JoJo's on U Street. Washington DC is renowned for its exceptional jazz acts, so this is a must-see, even if you are not a huge jazz enthusiast. You may find yourself becoming one after witnessing a phenomenal show by world-class musicians.

1ˢᵗ Day in Washington DC - Map

We have provided you with maps for all the recommended locations on your first day in Washington, D.C. These maps are available in Google Maps format, making it easy for you to use them on your smartphone or tablet while you explore the city.

Get this map online:
https://drive.google.com/open?id=1li6QCMTnfYETOsngsYLrmSiJCX0&usp=sharing

ZoomTip 1.1: Information on the White House

West Wing, which includes the Oval Office and offices for the President's staff, the East Wing, which contains the First Lady's office and the White House Social Secretary's office, and the Residence, which is the private living quarters for the President and their family.

While visiting the inside of the White House is very difficult, as it requires a submission three months in advance and approval from the White House Office of the Curator, visitors can still view the exterior of the building from the outside. It's recommended to take a tour or hire a guide to learn more about the history and significance of this iconic building.

To see the location of the White House and more information about it, please refer to ZoomTip 1.2.

ZoomTip 1.2: National Mall Museums and Monuments

The National Mall in Washington DC is a park located between the United States Capitol and the Lincoln Memorial. It contains many famous museums and monuments, making it one of the most visited places in the city. In this ZoomTip, we will highlight some of the must-see museums and monuments located in the National Mall.

National Air and Space Museum

The National Air and Space Museum is one of the most visited museums in the world, with over 8 million visitors per year. It contains the largest collection of historic aircraft and spacecraft in the world, including the original Wright Flyer, Charles Lindbergh's Spirit of St. Louis, and the Apollo 11 command module. The museum also features a planetarium and an IMAX theater.

The main building, which opened in 1976, is considered one of the best examples of modern architecture in the city. The museum has also been featured in popular movies such as A Night in the Museum 2.

Some of the most significant and captivating objects on display at the National Air and Space Museum include the Wright Flyer, the first airplane to achieve controlled, powered flight in 1903; one of the Douglas World Cruiser planes; a V-2 Rocket, the first human-made object to reach space; the Apollo 11 module; a sample of lunar rock; a rock from Mars; a Boeing B707 prototype; the Air France Concorde, a famous supersonic aircraft; and the Enola Gay, the plane used to drop the atomic bomb on Hiroshima in 1945.

Overall, the National Air and Space Museum is a must-visit attraction in Washington DC, particularly for aviation enthusiasts. With its incredible collection of air and space crafts, visitors are sure to be amazed. The best part? Admission to the museum is completely free.

World War II Memorial

The World War II Memorial is located on the National Mall and honors the 16 million Americans who served in the armed forces during World War II, including the more than 400,000 who gave their lives. The memorial consists of 56 pillars and a central plaza with a fountain, surrounded by 4,000 gold stars representing the more than 400,000 American lives lost during the war.

Washington Monument (obelisk)

The Washington Monument is an iconic obelisk located on the National Mall. It stands at 555 feet and is the tallest stone structure in the world.

Visitors can take an elevator to the top and enjoy stunning views of the city.

The Washington Monument is a prominent landmark located in the western part of the National Mall in Washington DC. This monument is a tribute to the first president of the United States, who played a crucial role in securing the country's independence during the War of Independence. Standing almost 170 meters tall, the monument is a stunning white obelisk made of granite, marble, and sandstone.

Designed by architect Robert Mills, construction of the monument began in 1848 and was completed in 1884. The monument's construction faced numerous challenges, including a lack of funds due to the Civil War that was taking place at the time. The two different types of marble used in the monument's construction can be seen after the 50-meter mark, which marks the two different phases of the monument's construction.

The Washington Monument is a symbol of respect and admiration for George Washington, who was greatly revered after the War of Independence. As the war master, he played a pivotal role in the country's victory, and his decisions to reject a salary and refuse the offer to become the king of the new country earned him widespread acclaim.

Lincoln Memorial

The Lincoln Memorial is a tribute to the 16th President of the United States, Abraham Lincoln. The memorial features a massive statue of Lincoln seated in contemplation, surrounded by 36 columns representing the states in the Union at the time of Lincoln's death. The location of the memorial was chosen because it is where Martin Luther King Jr. gave his famous "I Have a Dream" speech during the Civil Rights March on Washington in 1963.

The Lincoln Memorial is an iconic monument located on the National Mall in Washington DC, dedicated to the memory of former US President Abraham Lincoln. The building takes the form of a Greek Doric temple and features a striking 19-foot-tall statue of Lincoln seated in contemplation. Along with the statue, the memorial displays two of Lincoln's most famous speeches, the Gettysburg Address and his Second Inaugural Address. The monument has been the site of many historic events, including the famous "I Have a Dream" speech delivered by Martin Luther King Jr. during the Civil Rights March on Washington in 1963. Designed by architect Henry Bacon in the Beaux-Arts style, the Lincoln Memorial was completed in 1922 and has since become one of the most visited landmarks in the United States. The exterior of the monument features 36 columns, each standing at a height of 10 meters, and the names of the 48 states that existed at the time of construction are inscribed on the walls of the attic. Two additional commemorative plates were added for the states of Hawaii and Alaska after they joined the union. The Lincoln Memorial is managed by the National Park Service and is open to the public every day from 8 am until midnight, with the exception of Christmas Day.

Visitors to the National Mall can easily spend a full day exploring these and other museums and monuments in the area. Admission to most of the museums is free, although some special exhibits may require a fee. Don't forget to bring comfortable shoes and plenty of water, as the National Mall is a large and sprawling area to explore on foot.

2nd Day In Washington DC – Itinerary
9:00 AM

Start your day by having breakfast and heading back to the National Mall area to continue exploring the museums and monuments you couldn't visit on your first day. The National Air and Space Museum, the Hirshhorn Museum and Sculpture Garden, and the National Museum of the American Indian are some of the places you should consider visiting.

1:30 PM

Once you're done with the museums, take some time to visit the Lincoln Memorial and the National World War II Memorial, two of the most iconic monuments in the National Mall.

3:30 PM

Grab a bite to eat and head to Georgetown. You can take the 30N bus, which will take you to the heart of this historic neighborhood in less than half an hour. Walk around M Street, explore the colorful shops, and relax by the Potomac River.

6:00 PM

Return to your hotel or apartment and take a well-deserved break.

7:00 PM

Have dinner at one of the recommended restaurants in the Our Favorite Dining Places in Washington DC section.

9:00 PM

Take a final tour around the monuments area and see them beautifully illuminated at night. You can also enjoy a drink at a bar and experience the city's vibrant nightlife.

Map for Your Second Day in Washington DC

We have prepared a map that shows all the different activities we recommend for your second day in Washington DC. The map is available in Google Maps format, which you can easily access on your smartphone or tablet while you are in the city. Use it to navigate and

explore all the exciting places and activities we suggest for your second day in Washington DC.

Get this map online:

https://drive.google.com/open?id=17elIgQc1Z609B45U5GN4ZtOnQAs&usp=sharing

3rd Day in Washington DC – Itinerary

At **10:00**, start your day with a delicious breakfast and head to the Arlington Cemetery. Although technically located in a different state (Arlington, Virginia), this iconic military cemetery is a must-visit destination in the DC area. Established during the Recession War, the cemetery covers 624 hectares of land next to the Potomac River and is home to more than 250,000 graves of soldiers and veterans from all wars, including the Independence War and the War of Iraq. One of the most prominent individuals buried in Arlington Cemetery is former President John F. Kennedy. You'll also find several memorials worth visiting, such as the Challenger Shuttle monument, the Iwo Jima Memorial, and the 9/11 victims memorial.

To get to Arlington Cemetery, take the blue line on the metro up to the Arlington Cemetery station. While entrance to the cemetery is free, the journey may take a bit longer than other attractions located in the DC city center. However, the historic and somber ambiance of this landmark makes the trip well worth it.

13:30

Return to the Downtown area for lunch, using the same blue line metro that you used to get to Arlington Cemetery.

14:30

Visit the Thomas Jefferson Memorial, located next to the Potomac River. The monument was constructed in 1930 at the initiative of President Roosevelt, as Washington DC already had monuments to two other presidents: Lincoln and Washington. The Thomas Jefferson Memorial was inaugurated in 1943 and is faithful to Roman architecture. It is a circular building supported by two tall columns, and inside you'll find a bronze statue of Thomas Jefferson. Take some time to walk around the memorial and enjoy the scenic views of the Potomac River.

16:00

Return to your hotel or apartment to relax before your departure. Take this time to pack your luggage and prepare for your journey home. Afterwards, head to the airport to catch your flight.

3rd Day in Washington DC – Map

Below you will find the maps corresponding to all the different activities that we recommend for your third day in Washington DC. They are accessible in Google Maps format for you to easily use on your smartphone or tablet while you are in Washington.

Get this map online:

https://drive.google.com/open?id=1oSZ2vYmOGUq9okxzwA7dEvNOpUo&usp=sharing

13.Recommended Itineraries (3 to 7 Days)

How to Use These Itineraries

If you're planning a trip to Washington DC and are feeling a bit overwhelmed with all the things to see and do, don't worry! We've got you covered with these carefully crafted itineraries that will help you make the most of your time in the city.

To make the most of these itineraries, we recommend that you download the Google Maps app on your smartphone or tablet. This way, you can easily navigate to all the different places we recommend without getting lost or wasting time.

Each itinerary is broken down into different activities that you can do during the day. We've also included suggestions for where to eat and drink along the way. You'll find detailed information about each activity, including opening hours and entrance fees, so you can plan your day accordingly.

We've also included some helpful tips and information about each attraction to help you get the most out of your visit. For example, we've provided information about the White House and how to visit it, as well as details about the National Mall and its museums and monuments.

Whether you're a history buff, an art lover, or just looking to explore the city, these itineraries have something for everyone. So, grab your walking shoes, a water bottle, and get ready to discover the beauty and history of Washington DC!

Classic Washington, D.C. Highlights (3 Days)

In this itinerary, we have curated a three-day plan that covers the classic highlights of Washington, D.C. You will visit iconic monuments and memorials, explore the city's cultural institutions and museums, and take in the beauty of the Potomac River and the historic Georgetown neighborhood. Join us on this journey and discover the heart and soul of the nation's capital.

Day 1: Monuments, Memorials, and Museums

08:00 - Start your day with a hearty breakfast at Founding Farmers, located at 1924 Pennsylvania Ave NW, Washington, DC 20006.

09:00 - Head to the National Mall to see the monuments, memorials, and museums. Start with the Washington Monument and then proceed to the Lincoln Memorial. Don't forget to take a look at the reflecting pool and the World War II Memorial.

11:00 - Visit the National Museum of American History to learn about the history of the United States. Make sure to see the original Star-Spangled Banner and the First Ladies' Inaugural Gowns exhibit.

13:00 - Lunch at the National Museum of the American Indian's Mitsitam Cafe to enjoy Native American cuisine.

14:00 - Visit the National Air and Space Museum to see the original Wright Flyer, V-2 Rocket, Apollo 11 module, and the Boeing B707 prototype.

16:00 - Take a break at the Hirshhorn Museum and Sculpture Garden, which showcases modern and contemporary art.

18:00 - Dinner at The Hamilton, located at 600 14th St NW, Washington, DC 20005. This restaurant offers live music and a diverse menu.

20:00 - End your day with a nighttime tour of the monuments. See the memorials illuminated against the night sky. You can take a guided tour or walk around on your own.

Day 2: American History and Cultural Institutions

08:00 - Breakfast at Busboys and Poets, located at 2021 14th St NW, Washington, DC 20009. This restaurant offers a diverse menu and a bookstore.

09:00 - Start your day at the National Portrait Gallery to see the portraits of prominent figures in American history.

11:00 - Visit the United States Holocaust Memorial Museum to learn about the history of the Holocaust and its impact on the world.

13:00 - Lunch at the Mitsitam Cafe at the National Museum of the American Indian.

14:00 - Visit the Smithsonian American Art Museum to see the largest collection of American art in the world.

16:00 - Take a break at the National Gallery of Art to see works by Leonardo Da Vinci, Jan van Eyck, Rembrandt Van Rijn, and Vincent Van Gogh.

18:00 - Dinner at Founding Farmers, located at 1924 Pennsylvania Ave NW, Washington, DC 20006.

20:00 - Watch a show at the John F. Kennedy Center for the Performing Arts, located at 2700 F St NW, Washington, DC 20566. This performing arts center offers a variety of shows, including theater, dance, and music.

Day 3: Government Buildings and Scenic Georgetown

08:00 - Breakfast at Le Pain Quotidien, located at 2815 M St NW, Washington, DC 20007. This bakery offers a variety of pastries and breakfast items.

09:00 - Visit the United States Capitol to see where Congress meets and legislates. Take a guided tour of the Capitol or explore on your own.

11:00 - Head to the Library of Congress to see the world's largest library and its collection of books and manuscripts.

13:00 - Lunch at Baked & Wired, located at 1052 Thomas Jefferson St NW, Washington, DC 20007. This bakery offers a variety of sandwiches and desserts.

14:00 - Take a walk around the historic Georgetown neighborhood, known for its charming streets, colorful row houses, and boutique shops. Start at M Street, which is lined with popular shops, cafes, and restaurants. Stroll down the street and take in the vibrant atmosphere.

15:00 - Visit the Tudor Place Historic House and Garden, located at 1644 31st St NW, Washington, DC 20007. This National Historic Landmark offers a glimpse into the life of one of America's founding families. Explore the stunning gardens and take a guided tour of the house.

17:00 - Take a break at the Georgetown Waterfront Park, located at 3303 Water St NW, Washington, DC 20007. This park offers a peaceful escape from the hustle and bustle of the city. Relax by the water, take a walk along the boardwalk, or rent a kayak and explore the Potomac River.

19:00 - Dinner at Farmers Fishers Bakers, located at 3000 K St NW, Washington, DC 20007. This farm-to-table restaurant offers a variety of seafood dishes, as well as craft cocktails and local beer. Make sure to try the famous fish tacos.

21:00 - End the night at The Georgetown Piano Bar, located at 3287 M St NW, Washington, DC 20007. This cozy bar offers live music and a wide selection of drinks. Request your favorite song and sing along with the talented pianist.

23:00 - Return to your hotel or accommodation to rest and prepare for your departure the next day.

Family-Friendly Fun in the Capital (5 Days)

Washington, D.C. is an exciting and educational destination for families with children of all ages. From interactive museums to outdoor adventures and entertainment, there is something for everyone in the nation's capital. This itinerary provides a five-day plan for family-friendly fun in Washington, D.C. that includes visits to museums, zoos, parks, and more. Discover the city's rich history and culture while enjoying family bonding time in one of the most iconic cities in the United States.

Day 1: Interactive Museums and Playgrounds

08:00 - Start your day with breakfast at Founding Farmers located at 1924 Pennsylvania Ave NW, Washington, DC 20006. This farm-to-table restaurant offers a wide range of breakfast items.

09:00 - Visit the National Museum of American History, located at 1300 Constitution Ave NW, Washington, DC 20560. This museum has interactive exhibits and artifacts showcasing American history.

11:00 - Head to the National Building Museum, located at 401 F St NW, Washington, DC 20001. This museum has exhibits on architecture, design, and engineering, as well as a popular play area for kids called "The Building Zone."

13:00 - Enjoy lunch at Shake Shack, located at 1216 Connecticut Ave NW, Washington, DC 20036. This burger joint offers a variety of burgers, hot dogs, and shakes.

14:00 - Visit the Smithsonian National Air and Space Museum, located at Independence Ave SW, Washington, DC 20560. This museum has interactive exhibits showcasing the history of flight and space exploration.

16:00 - Spend the afternoon at the National Mall playground, located at 12th St NW & Jefferson Dr SW, Washington, DC 20004. This playground has a variety of equipment for kids of all ages.

18:00 - Have dinner at Jaleo, located at 480 7th St NW, Washington, DC 20004. This Spanish restaurant offers a variety of tapas and small plates.

Day 2: Zoos, Aquariums, and Nature Experiences

08:00 - Start your day with breakfast at Busboys and Poets, located at 2021 14th St NW, Washington, DC 20009. This restaurant offers a variety of breakfast items.

09:00 - Visit the National Zoological Park, located at 3001 Connecticut Ave NW, Washington, DC 20008. This zoo has a variety of animals, including pandas, elephants, and lions.

12:00 - Have lunch at the Mitsitam Cafe, located at 4th St & Independence Ave SW, Washington, DC 20560. This cafe offers a variety of Native American-inspired dishes.

13:00 - Visit the National Aquarium, located at 1401 Constitution Ave NW, Washington, DC 20230. This aquarium has a variety of marine life exhibits and interactive experiences.

15:00 - Spend the afternoon at the Kenilworth Park and Aquatic Gardens, located at 1550 Anacostia Ave NE, Washington, DC 20019. This park has beautiful gardens and a variety of aquatic plants and animals.

18:00 - Have dinner at the Eastern Market, located at 225 7th St SE, Washington, DC 20003. This market has a variety of food stalls and vendors.

Day 3: The National Mall and Beyond

08:00 - Start your day with breakfast at The Coupe, located at 3415 11th St NW, Washington, DC 20010. This restaurant offers a variety of breakfast items.

09:00 - Visit the United States Holocaust Memorial Museum, located at 100 Raoul Wallenberg Pl SW, Washington, DC 20024. This museum has exhibits and artifacts related to the Holocaust.

12:00 - Have lunch at the Mitsitam Native Foods Cafe, located at 4th St & Independence Ave SW, Washington, DC 20560. This cafe offers a variety of Native American-inspired dishes.

13:00 - Spend the afternoon at the National Mall, located at National Mall, Washington, DC 20565. This area is home to some of the most iconic monuments and museums in the country. Start by visiting the National Museum of American History, which has exhibits related to American history and culture.

16:00 - Head to the Tidal Basin for a scenic walk and view of the cherry blossom trees (if in season). This area also offers a great view of the Jefferson Memorial.

18:00 - Have dinner at Old Ebbitt Grill, located at 675 15th St NW, Washington, DC 20005. This historic restaurant has been serving customers since 1856 and offers a variety of classic American dishes.

20:00 - Catch a performance at the John F. Kennedy Center for the Performing Arts, located at 2700 F St NW, Washington, DC 20566. This iconic performing arts center has multiple theaters and hosts a variety of performances.

22:30 - End your day with a nightcap at the POV Rooftop Lounge and Terrace, located at 515 15th St NW, Washington, DC 20004. This rooftop bar offers stunning views of the city and a variety of cocktails.

Day 4: Outdoor Adventures and Parks

08:00 - Start your day with breakfast at Teaism, located at 400 8th St NW, Washington, DC 20004. This restaurant offers a variety of breakfast items and tea options.

09:00 - Head to Rock Creek Park, located at 3545 Williamsburg Ln NW, Washington, DC 20008. This park offers hiking trails, picnic areas, and a nature center.

12:00 - Have a picnic lunch in the park or grab lunch at the nearby Parkway Deli & Restaurant, located at 8317 Grubb Rd, Silver Spring, MD 20910. This deli offers a variety of sandwiches and classic Jewish deli items.

13:00 - Visit the National Arboretum, located at 3501 New York Ave NE, Washington, DC 20002. This park has a variety of gardens and exhibits related to plants and nature.

16:00 - Head to the National Mall and visit the National Museum of Natural History, which has exhibits related to natural history and science.

18:00 - Have dinner at Founding Farmers, located at 1924 Pennsylvania Ave NW, Washington, DC 20006. This farm-to-table restaurant offers a variety of American dishes.

20:00 - End your day with a visit to the Georgetown Waterfront Park, located at 3303 Water St NW, Washington, DC 20007. This park offers scenic views of the Potomac River and a great place to relax and unwind.

Day 5: Capital Entertainment and Dining

08:00 - Start your day with breakfast at Busboys and Poets, located at 2021 14th St NW, Washington, DC 20009. This restaurant offers a variety of breakfast items and coffee options.

09:30 - Head to the Newseum, located at 555 Pennsylvania Ave NW, Washington, DC 20001. This museum has exhibits related to news and journalism.

12:00 - Have lunch at District Taco, located at 1309 F St NW, Washington, DC 20004. This restaurant offers a variety of Mexican-inspired dishes.

13:00 - Visit the Smithsonian American Art Museum and the National Portrait Gallery, located at 8th St NW & F St NW, Washington, DC 20001. These museums have exhibits related to American art and culture.

16:00 - Head to the National Harbor, located at 165 Waterfront St, Oxon Hill, MD 20745. This waterfront area offers a variety of shopping, dining, and entertainment options.

18:00 - Have dinner at Fiola Mare, located at 310 0 K St NW, Washington, DC 20007. This restaurant offers upscale seafood dishes with waterfront views.

20:00 - End your trip with a visit to the Kennedy Center for the Performing Arts, located at 2700 F St NW, Washington, DC 20566. This performing arts center has a variety of shows and performances, including theater, dance, and music.

With this itinerary, you'll experience the best of family-friendly fun in the capital city. From interactive museums to outdoor adventures, there's something for everyone. Make sure to try some of the city's famous cuisine and explore its diverse neighborhoods. You'll leave with unforgettable memories and a newfound appreciation for all that Washington, D.C. has to offer.

Cultural Immersion in Washington, D.C. (7 Days)

Washington, D.C. is a city with a rich history and culture, making it an ideal destination for those seeking a cultural immersion experience. With seven days to explore, you can dive deep into the city's museums, monuments, and historic neighborhoods. This itinerary will take you through some of the most iconic landmarks and cultural institutions in the city, while also allowing you to discover some hidden gems that are off the beaten path. Get ready to immerse yourself in the art, history, and culture of Washington, D.C.

Day 1: The National Mall's Cultural Treasures

Welcome to Washington, D.C.! On your first day in the capital, we recommend exploring the cultural treasures of the National Mall. This iconic park is home to some of the country's most famous museums, monuments, and memorials, and is a must-visit for any first-time visitor to the city.

8:00 - Start your day with a delicious breakfast at Founding Farmers, located at 1924 Pennsylvania Ave NW, Washington, DC 20006. This farm-to-table restaurant offers a variety of breakfast options using locally-sourced ingredients.

9:00 - Begin your cultural journey with a visit to the Smithsonian National Museum of American History, located at 14th St NW & Constitution Ave NW, Washington, DC 20560. This museum showcases the country's history through a vast collection of artifacts, including the original Star-Spangled Banner, First Ladies' inaugural gowns, and the Greensboro Lunch Counter.

12:00 - Have lunch at the Mitsitam Native Foods Cafe, located at 4th St & Independence Ave SW, Washington, DC 20560. This cafe offers a variety of Native American-inspired dishes.

13:00 - After lunch, head to the National Museum of African American History and Culture, located at 1400 Constitution Ave NW, Washington, DC 20560. This museum is dedicated to exploring the African American experience through exhibits, artifacts, and interactive displays.

16:00 - Take a stroll along the Tidal Basin and visit the Franklin Delano Roosevelt Memorial, located at 1850 West Basin Dr SW, Washington, DC 20242. This beautiful monument honors the 32nd president and features a series of outdoor rooms representing different periods of Roosevelt's presidency.

18:00 - Have dinner at RPM Italian, located at 650 K St NW, Washington, DC 20001. This upscale restaurant offers a modern take on classic Italian cuisine.

20:00 - End your day with a visit to the Kennedy Center for the Performing Arts, located at 2700 F St NW, Washington, DC 20566. This iconic venue hosts a variety of performances, including music, theater, dance, and more.

Day 2: Off-the-Beaten-Path Museums and Galleries

On your second day in Washington, D.C., venture off the National Mall to discover the city's lesser-known museums and galleries. Start your day with breakfast at The Coupe, located in the Columbia Heights neighborhood. From there, head to the Phillips Collection, a museum of modern art located in the Dupont Circle neighborhood. The Phillips Collection features works by artists such as Renoir, Van Gogh, and Rothko.

Next, visit the National Museum of Women in the Arts, located in the downtown area. This museum features a collection of over 5,000 works of art created by women, including paintings, sculptures, and decorative arts.

For lunch, head to Union Market, a culinary marketplace featuring a variety of food vendors and specialty shops. Grab a bite to eat and explore the market's unique offerings.

After lunch, visit the Hirshhorn Museum and Sculpture Garden, located on the National Mall. This museum specializes in contemporary art and features works by artists such as Yoko Ono and Ai Weiwei.

End your day at the National Portrait Gallery and the Smithsonian American Art Museum, both located in the Chinatown neighborhood. The National Portrait Gallery features portraits of notable figures throughout American history, while the Smithsonian American Art Museum showcases American art from the colonial period to the present day.

In the evening, catch a performance at the nearby Ford's Theatre or head to the U Street Corridor for some live music and nightlife options.

Day 3: Performing Arts and Theatrical Experiences

Washington, D.C. is known for its vibrant performing arts scene, with a variety of theaters and venues showcasing everything from Broadway shows to experimental performances. Spend Day 3 exploring the city's theatrical offerings and immerse yourself in the world of the performing arts.

08:00 - Start your day with a hearty breakfast at Busboys and Poets, located at 2021 14th St NW, Washington, DC 20009. This restaurant offers a variety of breakfast items and coffee options.

09:30 - Visit the Kennedy Center for the Performing Arts, located at 2700 F St NW, Washington, DC 20566. Take a guided tour of the center's theaters and performance spaces, or check the schedule for any upcoming shows or events that interest you.

12:00 - Have lunch at the Roof Terrace Restaurant at the Kennedy Center, where you can enjoy delicious cuisine and stunning views of the Potomac River and the city.

14:00 - Explore the Shakespeare Theatre Company, located at 610 F St NW, Washington, DC 20004. Take a backstage tour of the theater or attend a performance of one of Shakespeare's classic plays.

16:00 - Head to the Arena Stage at the Mead Center for American Theater, located at 1101 6th St SW, Washington, DC 20024. This venue is known for its innovative productions and commitment to showcasing new and diverse voices in American theater.

18:00 - Enjoy dinner at Marcel's by Robert Wiedmaier, located at 2401 Pennsylvania Ave NW, Washington, DC 20037. This elegant French-Belgian restaurant offers a luxurious dining experience, complete with an extensive wine list and impeccable service.

20:00 - Finish the day with a performance at the Woolly Mammoth Theatre Company, located at 641 D St NW, Washington, DC 20004. This theater is known for its bold and boundary-pushing productions, showcasing the best in contemporary theater.

Day 4: Washington, D.C.'s Multicultural Neighborhoods

Experience the diverse and vibrant neighborhoods of Washington, D.C. on day four of your itinerary. From historic landmarks to eclectic shops and restaurants, each neighborhood offers a unique cultural experience.

8:00 - Start your day with breakfast at a local diner in the Shaw neighborhood. Try Florida Avenue Grill at 1100 Florida Ave NW, Washington, DC 20009, a beloved establishment that has been serving the community since 1944.

9:00 - Head to the U Street Corridor, also known as "Black Broadway," to explore the African American history and culture of the area. Visit the African American Civil War Memorial and Museum, located at 1925 Vermont Ave NW, Washington, DC 20001, to learn about the contributions of African American soldiers during the Civil War.

11:00 - Visit the National Museum of African American History and Culture, located at 1400 Constitution Ave NW, Washington, DC 20560. This museum showcases the African American experience, from slavery to present day.

1:00 - Have lunch at Ben's Chili Bowl, located at 1213 U St NW, Washington, DC 20009, a local institution famous for its chili half-smokes and history as a gathering place during the Civil Rights Movement.

2:00 - Explore the colorful and eclectic Adams Morgan neighborhood. Visit the LINE DC hotel, located at 1770 Euclid St NW, Washington, DC 20009, to see a unique blend of historic architecture and contemporary design.

4:00 - Take a short trip to the Dupont Circle neighborhood to visit the Phillips Collection, located at 1600 21st St NW, Washington, DC 20009. This museum features an impressive collection of modern and contemporary art.

7:00 - Have dinner at a Latin American restaurant in the lively Columbia Heights neighborhood, such as El Chucho at 3313 11th St NW,

Washington, DC 20010. Experience the flavors and culture of Latin America while enjoying the vibrant atmosphere of the neighborhood.

9:00 - End your day with a visit to the nearby Mount Pleasant neighborhood, known for its diverse community and artistic vibe. Grab a drink at one of the local bars or cafes, like The Raven Grill at 3125 Mount Pleasant St NW, Washington, DC 20010, and soak in the unique atmosphere of this multicultural neighborhood.

Day 5: Art, Music, and Literature Scene

On your fifth day in Washington, D.C., immerse yourself in the city's vibrant art, music, and literary scene. Start your day with breakfast at Busboys and Poets, a local favorite for its cozy atmosphere and community focus. After breakfast, head to the Hirshhorn Museum and Sculpture Garden, located on the National Mall. This contemporary art museum features a diverse collection of paintings, sculptures, and multimedia installations.

Next, explore the U Street Corridor, known as the "Black Broadway" for its rich history of African American music and culture. Visit the Duke Ellington Mural and the Lincoln Theatre, which has hosted legendary performers such as Ella Fitzgerald and Billie Holiday. Stop by the African American Civil War Museum to learn about the contributions of black soldiers during the Civil War.

For lunch, try some soul food at Oohhs & Aahhs, a popular local spot for comfort food like fried chicken and macaroni and cheese. After lunch, head to the National Museum of African American History and Culture, located on the National Mall. This museum tells the story of the African American experience through a powerful collection of artifacts, exhibits, and interactive displays.

In the afternoon, head to the Kennedy Center for the Performing Arts, located on the banks of the Potomac River. Take a guided tour of the center, which includes the Concert Hall, Opera House, and Eisenhower Theater. If you have time, catch a show or performance at one of the theaters.

End your day with a visit to the Library of Congress, the largest library in the world. Explore the Thomas Jefferson Building, which features stunning architecture and the iconic Main Reading Room. Browse the exhibits and collections, which include rare books, manuscripts, and prints.

For dinner, head to the iconic Old Ebbitt Grill, located just steps from the White House. This historic restaurant has been serving classic American cuisine since 1856 and has hosted a long list of famous patrons over the years. After dinner, catch a performance at the nearby Ford's Theatre, where Abraham Lincoln was assassinated in 1865. Today, the theater hosts a variety of plays, musicals, and performances throughout the year.

Day 6: Workshops, Classes, and Culinary Experiences

On the sixth day of your Washington, D.C. itinerary, you'll have the opportunity to participate in workshops, take classes, and explore the city's culinary scene. Start your day with a delicious breakfast at one of the city's many cafes, such as Baked & Wired in Georgetown or The Coupe in Columbia Heights.

After breakfast, head to one of the city's many cultural institutions to participate in a workshop or take a class. The Smithsonian Institution offers a variety of workshops and classes, including art classes at the Smithsonian American Art Museum and cooking classes at the National

Museum of the American Indian. You can also explore the art of storytelling at the Story District, which offers classes and workshops on various forms of storytelling.

For lunch, head to Union Market, located in the trendy Northeast neighborhood, to explore the city's culinary scene. This indoor market features a variety of food vendors and artisanal products, and offers cooking classes and workshops.

In the afternoon, continue your culinary adventure with a food tour. DC Metro Food Tours offers walking tours that explore the city's diverse food scene, from Ethiopian cuisine in the U Street Corridor to the international flavors of Adams Morgan. Alternatively, you can take a cooking class at the Hill Center at the Old Naval Hospital, which offers classes on everything from knife skills to pie-making.

As the evening approaches, unwind with a cocktail at one of the city's speakeasies, such as The Gibson or Harold Black. These hidden gems offer a cozy atmosphere and expertly-crafted cocktails. Alternatively, you can explore the city's live music scene at the legendary 9:30 Club or the intimate Black Cat.

End your day with a luxurious dinner at one of the city's Michelin-starred restaurants, such as The Inn at Little Washington or Sushi Taro. These restaurants offer a world-class culinary experience and impeccable service.

Day 7: D.C.'s Rich History and Architecture

On your final day in Washington, D.C., immerse yourself in the city's rich history and admire its stunning architecture. Here are some activities to consider:

8:00 - Start your day with breakfast at The Eastern Market, located at 225 7th St SE, Washington, DC 20003. This historic indoor market offers a variety of breakfast options, including fresh produce, baked goods, and prepared foods.

9:00 - Visit the National Museum of American History, located at 14th St & Constitution Ave NW, Washington, DC 20560. This museum has exhibits and artifacts related to American history and culture, including the original Star-Spangled Banner and the First Ladies' inaugural gowns.

12:00 - Have lunch at the Old Ebbitt Grill, located at 675 15th St NW, Washington, DC 20005. This iconic restaurant has been serving guests since 1856 and features classic American cuisine in a historic atmosphere.

2:00 - Take a walking tour of the historic Capitol Hill neighborhood, known for its stunning architecture and historic landmarks, including the U.S. Capitol and the Supreme Court.

5:00 - Visit the National Cathedral, located at 3101 Wisconsin Ave NW, Washington, DC 20016. This stunning Gothic cathedral is the sixth-largest in the world and features beautiful stained-glass windows and intricate stone carvings.

7:00 - End your day with dinner at The Hamilton, located at 600 14th St NW, Washington, DC 20005. This restaurant features a menu of American classics and live music performances in a beautifully restored space.

With its rich history and stunning architecture, Washington, D.C. offers a wealth of experiences to explore and enjoy. From museums and monuments to neighborhoods and restaurants, there's something for everyone to discover in this vibrant city.

Nature Lover's Washington, D.C. (4 Days)

Washington, D.C. is known for its impressive monuments, museums, and government buildings, but it also has plenty to offer for nature lovers. From parks and gardens to hiking trails and wildlife, this city has something for everyone who wants to escape the hustle and bustle of the city and immerse themselves in nature. In this itinerary, we have curated a list of the best outdoor activities and destinations in Washington, D.C. for a 4-day nature adventure. Get ready to explore the natural beauty of the nation's capital!

Day 1: Urban Parks and Green Spaces

08:00 - Start your day with a quick breakfast at The Coupe, located at 3415 11th St NW, Washington, DC 20010. This restaurant offers a variety of breakfast items to fuel up for a day in the great outdoors.

09:00 - Head to the National Mall, located at National Mall, Washington, DC 20565, and explore the many green spaces and urban parks in the area. Take a stroll around the Tidal Basin and admire the cherry blossoms in the spring or fall foliage in the autumn. Visit the Constitution Gardens, located at Constitution Ave NW & 17th St NW, Washington, DC 20001, which is a peaceful retreat in the heart of the city with a lake, walking paths, and plenty of wildlife.

12:00 - Grab a quick and healthy lunch at Sweetgreen, located at 221 Pennsylvania Ave SE, Washington, DC 20003. This salad chain offers fresh and organic ingredients to fuel your outdoor adventures.

13:00 - Visit the United States Botanic Garden, located at 100 Maryland Ave SW, Washington, DC 20001. This living plant museum is a great way to experience the beauty of nature in the city. Wander through the different gardens, including the rose garden, butterfly garden, and the jungle room.

15:00 - Take a leisurely walk through Meridian Hill Park, located at 16th St NW & W St NW, Washington, DC 20009. This park offers beautiful views of the city and is home to a cascading fountain, a historic statue, and plenty of green space to relax in.

18:00 - End your day with a relaxing dinner at Farmers Fishers Bakers, located at 3000 K St NW, Washington, DC 20007. This restaurant offers a farm-to-table menu with plenty of seafood options and an outdoor patio with waterfront views.

Day 2: Hiking, Biking, and Exploring Trails

Get ready for an active day as we explore the best hiking, biking, and trail options in Washington, D.C. Grab your comfortable shoes, a water bottle, and some sunscreen, and let's hit the trails!

8:00 - Start your day with a healthy breakfast at The Daily Dish, located at 8301 Grubb Rd, Silver Spring, MD 20910. This restaurant offers a variety of breakfast options, including vegan and gluten-free options.

9:00 - Head to Rock Creek Park, located at 5200 Glover Rd NW, Washington, DC 20015. This 1,754-acre park offers over 32 miles of hiking trails and is a favorite spot for local hikers and bikers. Spend the morning exploring the park's trails, including the popular Valley Trail and the Rock Creek Park Trail.

12:00 - Have a picnic lunch in the park with snacks and sandwiches from Wagshal's Market, located at 4845 Massachusetts Ave NW, Washington, DC 20016. This local market offers a variety of deli options, as well as grab-and-go snacks and drinks.

1:00 - After lunch, head to the Chesapeake and Ohio Canal National Historical Park, located at 1057 Thomas Jefferson St NW, Washington,

DC 20007. This 184.5-mile-long park offers hiking and biking trails along the Potomac River, including the popular Capital Crescent Trail. Rent a bike from the nearby Big Wheel Bikes and explore the trails at your own pace.

5:00 - After a day of hiking and biking, relax with a drink and some appetizers at Off the Record, located at 800 16th St NW, Washington, DC 20006. This upscale bar offers a variety of cocktails and small plates, and is a popular spot for locals and tourists alike.

7:00 - End your day with a delicious dinner at RPM Italian, located at 601 Massachusetts Ave NW, Washington, DC 20001. This Italian restaurant offers a variety of classic Italian dishes, as well as an extensive wine list.

Day 3: Water Activities and Wildlife Encounters

Washington, D.C. may be a bustling city, but it's also home to some beautiful bodies of water and the wildlife that inhabits them. On this day, you'll get to experience the natural side of the city from a different perspective as you explore the waterways and meet the animals that call them home.

8:00 - Start your day with a breakfast sandwich and coffee at The Coffee Bar, located at 1201 S St NW, Washington, DC 20009.

9:00 - Head to the Anacostia River, located in the southeastern part of the city. The river has been undergoing significant restoration efforts in recent years, and there are now plenty of opportunities to enjoy its natural beauty. Rent a kayak or paddleboard from one of the many outfitters in the area, such as Anacostia River Explorers, and spend the morning exploring the river and its surrounding wetlands.

12:00 - Have a picnic lunch at Kenilworth Park and Aquatic Gardens, located at 1550 Anacostia Ave NE, Washington, DC 20019. This unique park features beautiful water lilies and lotus flowers, as well as a variety of wildlife, such as turtles, frogs, and herons.

1:30 - After lunch, head to the National Zoological Park, located at 3001 Connecticut Ave NW, Washington, DC 20008. The zoo is home to over 2,700 animals from 390 different species, including giant pandas, elephants, and lions. Don't miss the American Trail exhibit, which features animals native to North America, such as sea otters and gray wolves.

5:00 - For dinner, head to The Salt Line, located at 79 Potomac Ave SE, Washington, DC 20003. This seafood-focused restaurant overlooks the Anacostia River and offers a variety of delicious dishes, such as lobster rolls and clam chowder.

7:00 - End your day by attending a performance at The Anthem, located at 901 Wharf St SW, Washington, DC 20024. This state-of-the-art music venue features a wide range of acts, from indie bands to internationally renowned artists. Check their schedule and book your tickets in advance to ensure you don't miss out on the fun.

Day 4: Gardens, Arboretums, and Conservation Areas

On the fourth day of your nature lover's adventure in Washington, D.C., you'll explore the city's beautiful gardens, arboretums, and conservation areas.

08:00 - Start your day with breakfast at Teaism, located at 800 Connecticut Ave NW, Washington, DC 20006. This restaurant offers a variety of breakfast items, including Japanese-inspired options.

09:00 - Visit the United States Botanic Garden, located at 100 Maryland Ave SW, Washington, DC 20001. This garden features a variety of plants and flowers from around the world, as well as a conservatory with seasonal exhibits.

11:00 - Head to the National Arboretum, located at 3501 New York Ave NE, Washington, DC 20002. This expansive park features a variety of gardens and collections, including a bonsai museum and a grove of state trees.

13:00 - Have lunch at Mitsitam Cafe, located at 4th St & Independence Ave SW, Washington, DC 20560. This cafe offers a variety of Native American-inspired dishes using seasonal and locally-sourced ingredients.

14:00 - Visit the Kenilworth Aquatic Gardens, located at 1550 Anacostia Ave NE, Washington, DC 20019. This park features beautiful water gardens with lily pads, lotus flowers, and aquatic wildlife.

16:00 - Head to the Rock Creek Park Nature Center and Planetarium, located at 5200 Glover Rd NW, Washington, DC 20015. This center features interactive exhibits on the park's wildlife and natural history, as well as a planetarium with shows for all ages.

18:00 - Have dinner at Brookland's Finest Bar & Kitchen, located at 3126 12th St NE, Washington, DC 20017. This restaurant offers American comfort food with a focus on seasonal and locally-sourced ingredients.

Culinary Tour of the Capital (3 Days)

Embark on a culinary adventure in the nation's capital with our three-day itinerary, designed to showcase the best of Washington, D.C.'s diverse food scene. From upscale dining to casual street fare, this itinerary offers something for every taste and budget. Indulge in the flavors of the city as you explore unique neighborhoods, sample regional cuisine, and discover hidden gems in the local culinary landscape. Get ready to satisfy your taste buds and experience the delicious side of Washington, D.C.

Day 1: Iconic D.C. Eateries and Food Traditions

08:00 - Start your day with breakfast at Ben's Chili Bowl, located at 1213 U St NW, Washington, DC 20009. This iconic D.C. eatery has been serving up its famous chili dogs and half-smokes since 1958.

09:00 - Head to Eastern Market, located at 225 7th St SE, Washington, DC 20003. This historic indoor/outdoor market has been a hub for local food and artisanal goods since 1873.

12:00 - Have lunch at Old Ebbitt Grill, located at 675 15th St NW, Washington, DC 20005. This historic restaurant, established in 1856, is known for its classic American cuisine and oyster bar.

14:00 - Visit the National Museum of American History, located at 1300 Constitution Ave NW, Washington, DC 20560. This museum has exhibits related to American history and culture, including food and drink traditions.

18:00 - Have dinner at The Palm, located at 1225 19th St NW, Washington, DC 20036. This upscale steakhouse has been a D.C. institution since 1972, serving up classic American dishes and signature cocktails.

Day 2: International Cuisine and Diverse Dining

08:00 - Start your day with breakfast at A Baked Joint, located at 440 K St NW, Washington, DC 20001. This bakery offers a variety of breakfast items and coffee options.

09:30 - Head to the Union Market, located at 1309 5th St NE, Washington, DC 20002. This indoor market features a variety of international cuisine and artisanal goods.

12:00 - Have lunch at Ambar, located at 523 8th St SE, Washington, DC 20003. This Balkan restaurant offers a unique dining experience with small plates and bottomless brunch options.

14:00 - Visit the National Museum of African American History and Culture, located at 1400 Constitution Ave NW, Washington, DC 20560. This museum has exhibits related to African American history and culture, including food and culinary traditions.

18:00 - Have dinner at Rose's Luxury, located at 717 8th St SE, Washington, DC 20003. This award-winning restaurant offers a seasonal menu with global flavors and a relaxed atmosphere.

Day 3: Sustainable Dining and Craft Beverage Experiences

08:00 - Start your day with breakfast at Founding Farmers, located at 1924 Pennsylvania Ave NW, Washington, DC 20006. This farm-to-table restaurant offers a variety of breakfast options using locally-sourced ingredients.

09:30 - Head to the Wharf, located at 760 Maine Ave SW, Washington, DC 20024. This waterfront area features a variety of sustainable seafood options and craft beverage experiences.

12:00 - Have lunch at Busboys and Poets, located at 450 K St NW, Washington, DC 20001. This restaurant offers a diverse menu with vegetarian and vegan options, as well as a focus on community and social justice.

14:00 - Visit the New Columbia Distillers, located at 1832 Fenwick St NE, Washington, DC 20002. This craft distillery produces Green Hat Gin, a local favorite.

18:00 - Have dinner at The Dabney, located at 122 Blagden Alley NW, Washington, DC 20001. This Michelin-starred restaurant features a seasonal menu with a focus on locally-sourced ingredients and wood-fired cooking techniques.

20:00 - End your culinary tour with a nightcap at the Columbia Room, located at 124 Blagden Alley NW, Washington, DC 20001. This award-winning bar offers craft cocktails made with locally-sourced ingredients and a focus on sustainability.

With your taste buds fully satisfied and a newfound appreciation for the diverse culinary landscape of Washington, D.C., it's time to bid farewell to the nation's capital.

Washington, D.C. on a Budget (5 Days)

If you're looking to explore the nation's capital without breaking the bank, you're in luck! Washington, D.C. is home to a plethora of free attractions, making it an ideal destination for budget travelers. With this itinerary, you can discover the best of D.C.'s historic landmarks, cultural institutions, and scenic parks, all while keeping your wallet happy. So pack your bags and get ready for a five-day adventure in Washington, D.C. on a budget!

Day 1: Free Attractions and Affordable Adventures

08:00 - Start your day with breakfast at Ted's Bulletin, located at 1818 14th St NW, Washington, DC 20009. This diner-style restaurant offers a variety of breakfast items at affordable prices.

09:30 - Visit the National Mall, located at National Mall, Washington, DC 20565. This area is home to many free attractions, including the Lincoln Memorial, Washington Monument, and World War II Memorial.

12:00 - Have lunch at Ben's Chili Bowl, located at 1213 U St NW, Washington, DC 20009. This iconic eatery offers affordable chili dogs and other classic American fare.

13:30 - Take a free tour of the United States Bureau of Engraving and Printing, located at 14th St SW & C St SW, Washington, DC 20228. This tour shows the process of printing US currency and is a unique and interesting experience.

15:30 - Head to the National Gallery of Art, located at 6th St & Constitution Ave NW, Washington, DC 20565. This museum offers free admission to its permanent collection, featuring works by artists such as da Vinci, Rembrandt, and Van Gogh.

18:00 - Have dinner at &pizza, located at 1250 U St NW, Washington, DC 20009. This fast-casual pizza chain offers customizable pizzas at affordable prices.

Day 2: Budget-Friendly Museums and Cultural Experiences

08:00 - Start your day with breakfast at The Coupe, located at 3415 11th St NW, Washington, DC 20010. This restaurant offers a variety of breakfast items at reasonable prices.

09:30 - Visit the Smithsonian American Art Museum and the National Portrait Gallery, located at 8th St NW & F St NW, Washington, DC 20001. These museums offer free admission to their permanent collections, featuring American art and culture.

12:00 - Have lunch at the Mitsitam Native Foods Cafe, located at 4th St & Independence Ave SW, Washington, DC 20560. This cafe offers affordable Native American-inspired dishes.

13:30 - Take a free tour of the United States Capitol, located at East Capitol St NE & First St SE, Washington, DC 20004. This tour provides insight into the history and workings of the US government.

16:00 - Head to the Georgetown neighborhood, located at 1228 Wisconsin Ave NW, Washington, DC 20007. This area offers affordable shopping and dining options, as well as historic architecture and scenic views of the Potomac River.

18:00 - Have dinner at Surfside, located at 2444 Wisconsin Ave NW, Washington, DC 20007. This restaurant offers affordable tacos, burritos, and other Mexican-inspired dishes.

Day 3: Inexpensive Dining and Entertainment

08:00 - Start your day with breakfast at Ted's Bulletin, located at 1818 14th St NW, Washington, DC 20009. This diner-style restaurant offers a variety of breakfast items at affordable prices.

09:00 - Head to the U Street Corridor, located at U St NW, Washington, DC 20009. This historic neighborhood features a variety of street art, music venues, and small businesses to explore.

12:00 - Have lunch at Ben's Chili Bowl, located at 1213 U St NW, Washington, DC 20009. This iconic diner has been serving up its famous chili dogs and half-smokes since 1958.

13:00 - Take a self-guided walking tour of the Shaw neighborhood, located just north of U Street. This area has a rich history and features a variety of historic landmarks and murals.

16:00 - Visit the National Postal Museum, located at 2 Massachusetts Ave NE, Washington, DC 20002. This free museum has exhibits and artifacts related to the history of the U.S. Postal Service.

18:00 - Have dinner at &pizza, located at 1118 H St NE, Washington, DC 20002. This fast-casual pizza chain offers customizable pies at affordable prices.

Day 4: Outdoor Fun and Natural Beauty

08:00 - Start your day with breakfast at The Coupe, located at 3415 11th St NW, Washington, DC 20010. This restaurant offers a variety of breakfast items at affordable prices.

09:00 - Head to Rock Creek Park, located at 5200 Glover Rd NW, Washington, DC 20015. This urban park features a variety of hiking trails and outdoor activities.

12:00 - Have lunch at Meats & Foods, located at 247 Florida Ave NW, Washington, DC 20001. This butcher shop and deli offers a variety of sandwiches and salads at reasonable prices.

13:00 - Rent bikes from Capital Bikeshare and explore the city on two wheels. Bikes can be rented from various locations throughout the city and are an affordable way to see the sights.

18:00 - Have dinner at Cava Mezze, located at 527 8th St SE, Washington, DC 20003. This Mediterranean restaurant offers a variety of small plates at affordable prices.

Day 5: Neighborhood Explorations and Street Art

08:00 - Start your day with breakfast at Old Ebbitt Grill, located at 675 15th St NW, Washington, DC 20005. This historic restaurant offers a variety of breakfast options at reasonable prices.

09:00 - Visit the Lincoln Memorial, located at 2 Lincoln Memorial Cir NW, Washington, DC 20037. This iconic landmark is free to visit and offers stunning views of the National Mall.

12:00 - Have lunch at District Taco, located at 1309 F St NW, Washington, DC 20004. This Mexican restaurant offers a variety of tacos and burritos at affordable prices.

13:00 - Visit the National Museum of American History, located at 14th St and Constitution Ave NW, Washington, DC 20001. This free museum has exhibits and artifacts related to American history and culture.

16:00 - Take a self-guided walking tour of the Capitol Hill neighborhood, located east of the National Mall. This area features a variety of historic landmarks and charming row houses.

18:00 - Have dinner at Busboys and Poets, located at 2021 14th St NW, Washington, DC 20009. This restaurant offers a diverse menu with vegetarian and vegan

Luxurious Washington, D.C. Getaway (4 Days)

Indulge in the ultimate luxurious experience with a four-day getaway to Washington, D.C. This itinerary is tailored to those seeking the finest accommodations, dining, and activities the city has to offer. From high-end shopping to spa treatments, every detail has been carefully selected to provide a luxurious escape. Explore the city's historic landmarks and cultural attractions in style, and unwind in luxurious accommodations at night. Get ready for a truly opulent adventure in the nation's capital.

Day 1: Upscale Hotels and Fine Dining

08:00 - Arrive in style and check-in to the luxurious Four Seasons Hotel Washington, D.C., located at 2800 Pennsylvania Ave NW, Washington, DC 20007. This five-star hotel boasts elegant accommodations, a full-service spa, and fine dining at the Michelin-starred Bourbon Steak restaurant.

12:00 - Have a leisurely lunch at the upscale Fiola, located at 601 Pennsylvania Ave NW, Washington, DC 20004. This Italian-inspired restaurant features an extensive wine list and a menu that highlights locally-sourced ingredients.

14:00 - Take a private tour of the National Gallery of Art, located at 6th St and Constitution Ave NW, Washington, DC 20565. This exclusive experience offers a personalized tour of the museum's renowned art collection.

18:00 - Enjoy a sophisticated dinner at Marcel's by Robert Wiedmaier, located at 2401 Pennsylvania Ave NW, Washington, DC 20037. This upscale French-Belgian restaurant features a prix fixe menu and an extensive wine list.

Day 2: Exclusive Tours and Private Experiences

08:00 - Start your day with breakfast at the hotel's Seasons Restaurant, featuring seasonal American cuisine and a serene atmosphere.

10:00 - Take a private tour of the U.S. Capitol building, located at East Capitol St NE & First St SE, Washington, DC 20004. This exclusive experience allows you to explore the historic building at your own pace with a personal guide.

12:00 - Have a private lunch at The Source by Wolfgang Puck, located at 575 Pennsylvania Ave NW, Washington, DC 20001. This upscale restaurant features a contemporary Asian-inspired menu and a sleek, modern atmosphere.

14:00 - Visit the exclusive shops at CityCenterDC, located at 825 10th St NW, Washington, DC 20001. This high-end shopping destination features luxury retailers such as Louis Vuitton and Gucci.

18:00 - Take a private sunset cruise on the Potomac River, featuring stunning views of the city's landmarks and a romantic atmosphere.

Day 3: High-End Shopping and Elegant Entertainment

08:00 - Start your day with breakfast at Le Diplomate, located at 1601 14th St NW, Washington, DC 20009. This French brasserie features a classic menu and a charming Parisian atmosphere.

10:00 - Shop for luxury goods at the upscale stores in Georgetown, such as Tuckernuck and Rag & Bone.

12:00 - Have a sophisticated lunch at the elegant Rose's Luxury, located at 717 8th St SE, Washington, DC 20003. This Michelin-starred restaurant features a creative menu and a stylish, relaxed atmosphere.

14:00 - Visit the John F. Kennedy Center for the Performing Arts, located at 2700 F St NW, Washington, DC 20566. This iconic performing arts venue offers a range of shows and events featuring world-renowned artists.

18:00 - Enjoy an elegant dinner at the award-winning Blue Duck Tavern, located at 1201 24th St NW, Washington, DC 20037. This farm-to-table restaurant features a seasonal menu and an inviting atmosphere.

Day 4: Spa Retreats and Indulgent Relaxation

08:00 - Start your day with breakfast in bed, courtesy of the hotel's room service.

09:00 - Spend the morning relaxing and rejuvenating at the hotel's spa. Treat yourself to a massage, facial, or other spa services.

12:00 - Have a leisurely lunch at The Spa at Mandarin Oriental, located at 1330 Maryland Ave SW, Washington, DC 20024. This spa offers a healthy spa cuisine menu for guests to enjoy.

14:00 - After lunch, continue your pampering with a manicure or pedicure at one of the city's high-end nail salons, such as Nailsaloon or Polished.

17:00 - End your luxurious getaway with a sunset champagne cruise on the Potomac River, offered by companies such as Potomac Riverboat Company or Capital Yacht Charters. Enjoy stunning views of the city skyline while sipping on bubbly and indulging in hors d'oeuvres.

Washington, D.C. for the Solo Traveler (5 Days)

Washington, D.C. is a city with so much to offer, from historical landmarks to cultural institutions to world-class dining and entertainment. And for solo travelers, it can be an excellent destination to explore on your own terms. With a mix of independent exploration and social activities, this itinerary is designed to help you get the most out of your solo trip to the nation's capital. Whether you're interested in history, culture, food, or nightlife, there's something for everyone in Washington, D.C. So pack your bags, put on your walking shoes, and get ready for a memorable solo adventure in this vibrant city.

Day 1: Guided Tours and Networking Opportunities

08:00 - Start your day with breakfast at The Potter's House, located at 1658 Columbia Rd NW, Washington, DC 20009. This community cafe offers a variety of breakfast items and coffee options, as well as a space for networking and socializing.

09:30 - Join a guided walking tour of the National Mall and its monuments, offered by companies such as Free Tours by Foot or DC by Foot. This is a great way to see the iconic sites of D.C. while meeting other travelers.

12:00 - Have lunch at Union Market, located at 1309 5th St NE, Washington, DC 20002. This food hall features a variety of local vendors offering everything from seafood to sushi to BBQ.

14:00 - Visit the Smithsonian American Art Museum and the National Portrait Gallery, located at 8th St NW & F St NW, Washington, DC 20001. These museums have exhibits related to American art and culture, and offer a chance to explore at your own pace.

18:00 - Attend a networking event or meetup in D.C., such as those hosted by groups like DC Tech Meetup or Washington D.C. Young

Professionals. This is a great opportunity to connect with locals and other travelers.

Day 2: Exploring D.C.'s Unique Neighborhoods

08:00 - Start your day with breakfast at The Coupe, located at 3415 11th St NW, Washington, DC 20010. This restaurant offers a variety of breakfast items.

09:30 - Take a self-guided walking tour of D.C.'s unique neighborhoods, such as Georgetown, Dupont Circle, or Adams Morgan. These areas are full of historic architecture, trendy boutiques, and charming cafes.

12:00 - Have lunch at Ben's Chili Bowl, located at 1213 U St NW, Washington, DC 20009. This iconic D.C. eatery is famous for its chili dogs and half-smokes.

14:00 - Visit the National Museum of African American History and Culture, located at 1400 Constitution Ave NW, Washington, DC 20560. This museum has exhibits and artifacts related to the African American experience in the United States.

18:00 - Have dinner at a trendy restaurant in one of D.C.'s up-and-coming neighborhoods, such as Shaw or H Street.

Day 3: Museums, Galleries, and Cultural Experiences

08:00 - Start your day with breakfast at Founding Farmers, located at 1924 Pennsylvania Ave NW, Washington, DC 20006. This farm-to-table restaurant offers a variety of breakfast options using locally-sourced ingredients.

09:30 - Visit the National Museum of African American History and Culture, located at 1400 Constitution Ave NW, Washington, DC 20560.

This museum showcases the history and culture of African Americans in the United States.

12:00 - Have lunch at the Mitsitam Native Foods Cafe, located at 4th St & Independence Ave SW, Washington, DC 20560. This cafe offers a variety of Native American-inspired dishes.

13:00 - Explore the National Gallery of Art, located at 6th St and Constitution Ave NW, Washington, DC 20565. This art museum features an extensive collection of American and European art, including works by Da Vinci, Rembrandt, and Monet.

16:00 - Take a stroll through the scenic Georgetown neighborhood, known for its charming architecture, quaint shops and cafes, and stunning views of the Potomac River.

19:00 - Have dinner at Fiola Mare, located at 3100 K St NW, Washington, DC 20007. This upscale Italian seafood restaurant offers stunning waterfront views and a menu featuring fresh, locally-sourced ingredients.

Day 4: Active Adventures and Outdoor Fun

08:00 - Start your day with breakfast at The Coupe, located at 3415 11th St NW, Washington, DC 20010. This restaurant offers a variety of breakfast items.

09:30 - Rent a bike from Capital Bikeshare and explore the scenic C&O Canal Towpath, a historic canal towpath that stretches 184.5 miles from Georgetown to Cumberland, Maryland.

12:00 - Have a picnic lunch at Rock Creek Park, a beautiful urban park located in the heart of D.C.

14:00 - Visit the Smithsonian's National Zoo, located at 3001 Connecticut Ave NW, Washington, DC 20008. This zoo is home to over 2,700 animals, representing nearly 400 species. You can observe giant pandas, lions, tigers, gorillas, and many more animals in their habitats. The zoo also offers various events and activities, such as animal encounters and behind-the-scenes tours, which can enhance your experience.

18:00 - Head to U Street Corridor, located in the Northwest quadrant of D.C., for some evening entertainment. This neighborhood has a vibrant nightlife scene and is known for its live music venues, bars, and restaurants. Enjoy some local craft beer at the Brixton or listen to some jazz at the famous Bohemian Caverns.

20:00 - Have dinner at Le Diplomate, located at 1601 14th St NW, Washington, DC 20009. This French brasserie serves classic French dishes, such as steak frites and coq au vin, in a stylish and sophisticated atmosphere.

22:00 - End the night with a nightcap at the POV rooftop bar, located at 515 15th St NW, Washington, DC 20004. This bar offers stunning views of the city and a chic ambiance. Enjoy a signature cocktail while taking in the panoramic skyline of the nation's capital.

Day 5: Nightlife and Social Events

After a few days of exploring nature and taking in the sights and sounds of Washington, D.C., it's time to experience the city's vibrant nightlife scene. This itinerary is all about enjoying the city's bars, restaurants, and social events. Get ready to sample delicious food and drinks, dance the night away, and make new friends.

8:00 pm - Start your night with a cocktail at the rooftop bar of the W Washington D.C., located at 515 15th St NW, Washington, DC 20004. Enjoy stunning views of the city and sip on expertly-crafted cocktails.

9:30 pm - Head to Adams Morgan, a trendy neighborhood known for its diverse nightlife scene. Grab dinner at one of the many restaurants on 18th Street NW, such as Mintwood Place or Smoke & Barrel.

11:00 pm - Check out the music scene at the 9:30 Club, located at 815 V St NW, Washington, DC 20001. This iconic venue has hosted some of the biggest names in music and is a must-visit for any music lover.

1:00 am - End your night at the POV rooftop lounge at the W Washington D.C. This upscale bar offers stunning views of the White House and the city skyline, as well as a wide selection of drinks and snacks.

If you're looking for more low-key options, head to the U Street Corridor for a wide selection of bars and lounges, or check out the H Street Corridor for a more eclectic vibe. Whatever your preference, Washington, D.C. has a nightlife scene that is sure to satisfy.

Romantic Washington, D.C. Escape (3 Days)

Escape with your loved one to the charming city of Washington, D.C. and indulge in a romantic getaway filled with enchanting sights and unforgettable experiences. From strolling through picturesque neighborhoods to dining at intimate restaurants, this three-day itinerary is designed to help you create lasting memories with your special someone. Explore the city's rich history, culture, and natural beauty, and let the magic of Washington, D.C. bring you closer together.

Day 1: Intimate Dining and Sunset Strolls

08:00 - Start your day with breakfast at Le Diplomate, located at 1601 14th St NW, Washington, DC 20009. This French cafe offers a variety of breakfast dishes and pastries.

09:00 - Take a leisurely stroll through Meridian Hill Park, located at 2400 15th St NW, Washington, DC 20008. Enjoy the park's beautiful fountains, gardens, and sculptures.

11:00 - Head to the Smithsonian American Art Museum, located at 8th St NW & F St NW, Washington, DC 20001. This museum has a collection of American art and is a great spot for a romantic date.

13:00 - Have lunch at Rasika, located at 633 D St NW, Washington, DC 20004. This Michelin-starred Indian restaurant offers a delicious menu of modern Indian cuisine.

15:00 - Explore the U.S. Botanic Garden, located at 100 Maryland Ave SW, Washington, DC 20001. This beautiful garden is perfect for a romantic afternoon stroll.

18:00 - Have dinner at The Red Hen, located at 1822 1st St NW, Washington, DC 20001. This Italian-inspired restaurant is known for its farm-to-table dishes and cozy ambiance.

20:00 - Take a sunset walk along the Tidal Basin, located at 1501 Maine Ave SW, Washington, DC 20024. Enjoy the beautiful views of the Jefferson Memorial and the Potomac River.

22:00 - End your day with a nightcap at the POV Rooftop Lounge and Terrace, located at 515 15th St NW, Washington, DC 20004. This rooftop bar offers stunning views of the city and delicious cocktails.

Day 2: Romantic Sightseeing and Cultural Experiences

8:00 - Enjoy breakfast in bed at your hotel or indulge in a romantic breakfast at Bistro Bis, located at 15 E St NW, Washington, DC 20001. This charming French restaurant offers a delightful breakfast menu and intimate atmosphere.

9:00 - Head to the National Mall and take a stroll through the picturesque Tidal Basin, enjoying views of the Jefferson Memorial, Martin Luther King Jr. Memorial, and the cherry blossom trees.

11:00 - Take a tour of the historic mansion and gardens at Dumbarton Oaks, located at 1703 32nd St NW, Washington, DC 20007. This stunning estate boasts a collection of Byzantine and Pre-Columbian art, as well as a romantic garden.

1:00 - Have lunch at the intimate Rose's Luxury, located at 717 8th St SE, Washington, DC 20003. This cozy restaurant offers a variety of seasonal dishes and a welcoming atmosphere.

2:30 - Explore the romantic Phillips Collection, located at 1600 21st St NW, Washington, DC 20009. This museum features an impressive collection of impressionist and modern art, as well as special exhibitions.

4:30 - Enjoy a relaxing couples massage at the Spa at Mandarin Oriental, located at 1330 Maryland Ave SW, Washington, DC 20024. This luxurious spa offers a variety of treatments designed to help you unwind and connect with your partner.

7:00 - Savor a romantic dinner at Fiola Mare, located at 3100 K St NW Suite 101, Washington, DC 20007. This waterfront restaurant features exquisite Italian seafood dishes and stunning views of the Potomac River.

9:00 - Catch a show at the intimate Kennedy Center's Millennium Stage, located at 2700 F St NW, Washington, DC 20566. This venue offers free performances every day, ranging from music to dance to theater.

11:00 - End the evening with a nightcap at the cozy Columbia Room, located at 124 Blagden Alley NW, Washington, DC 20001. This speakeasy-style bar offers a wide selection of classic cocktails and a cozy, romantic atmosphere.

Day 3: Relaxing Couples' Activities and Evening Entertainment

8:00 AM - Start your day with a leisurely breakfast in bed at the Line DC hotel. Enjoy a selection of pastries, coffee, and other breakfast items from the hotel's room service menu.

9:00 AM - Head to the spa at the Mandarin Oriental, located at 1330 Maryland Ave SW, Washington, DC 20024. Indulge in a couples massage or other spa treatments to help you relax and unwind.

11:00 AM - Visit the National Gallery of Art, located at 6th and Constitution Ave NW, Washington, DC 20565. Explore the museum's collection of art from around the world, including paintings, sculptures, and other works of art.

1:00 PM - Have lunch at the rooftop bar at the W Hotel, located at 515 15th St NW, Washington, DC 20004. Enjoy stunning views of the city skyline while you dine on a selection of small plates and cocktails.

2:30 PM - Take a stroll through the U.S. Botanic Garden, located at 100 Maryland Ave SW, Washington, DC 20001. Admire the colorful flowers and plants, and relax in the peaceful setting of this urban oasis.

4:00 PM - Visit the Phillips Collection, located at 1600 21st St NW, Washington, DC 20009. This intimate museum features a collection of modern and contemporary art, including works by Picasso, Van Gogh, and other renowned artists.

6:00 PM - Have dinner at Iron Gate, located at 1734 N St NW, Washington, DC 20036. This restaurant offers a romantic and intimate setting, with a menu of Mediterranean-inspired dishes made from locally-sourced ingredients.

8:00 PM - Catch a show at the Kennedy Center for the Performing Arts, located at 2700 F St NW, Washington, DC 20566. Choose from a variety of performances, including theater, ballet, opera, and more.

10:00 PM - End your evening with a nightcap at the POV rooftop bar at the W Hotel, located at 515 15th St NW, Washington, DC 20004. Enjoy panoramic views of the city while sipping on cocktails and reflecting on your romantic escape in Washington, D.C.

Accessible Washington, D.C. (4 Days)

Washington, D.C. is a city full of history, culture, and attractions, and it offers something for everyone, including those with mobility challenges. This accessible itinerary is designed to help travelers with disabilities or limited mobility experience the best of what the city has to offer. From accessible museums to wheelchair-friendly tours, this four-day itinerary includes some of the most accessible attractions in Washington, D.C. and offers tips for getting around the city with ease.

Day 1: Accessible Attractions and Tours

08:00 - Start your day with breakfast at Founding Farmers, located at 1924 Pennsylvania Ave NW, Washington, DC 20006. This farm-to-table restaurant offers a variety of breakfast options using locally-sourced ingredients.

09:00 - Visit the Smithsonian Institution National Museum of American History, located at 1400 Constitution Ave NW, Washington, DC 20560.

The museum is fully accessible and has exhibits related to American history and culture.

11:00 - Take an accessible tour of the United States Capitol Building. The Capitol Visitor Center offers a variety of tour options for visitors with disabilities, including sign language interpretation and wheelchair accessibility.

13:00 - Have lunch at The Source by Wolfgang Puck, located at 575 Pennsylvania Ave NW, Washington, DC 20001. This restaurant offers a contemporary Asian-inspired menu and is fully accessible.

14:30 - Visit the National Gallery of Art, located at 6th and Constitution Ave NW, Washington, DC 20565. The museum is fully accessible and has a large collection of art from around the world.

17:00 - Head to the Kennedy Center for the Performing Arts, located at 2700 F St NW, Washington, DC 20566. The Kennedy Center offers accessible performances and tours for visitors with disabilities.

19:00 - Have dinner at Oyamel Cocina Mexicana, located at 401 7th St NW, Washington, DC 20004. This restaurant offers a range of authentic Mexican dishes and is fully accessible.

21:00 - Take a stroll around the Tidal Basin and see the illuminated memorials at night. The walkway is fully accessible and offers stunning views of the monuments.

Day 2: Inclusive Museums and Cultural Institutions

08:00 - Start your day with breakfast at Busboys and Poets, located at 2021 14th St NW, Washington, DC 20009. This restaurant offers a variety of breakfast items and coffee options.

09:00 - Visit the Smithsonian American History Museum, located at 1400 Constitution Ave NW, Washington, DC 20560. This museum offers accessible exhibits that showcase the history and culture of the United States.

11:00 - Head to the Hirshhorn Museum and Sculpture Garden, located at Independence Ave SW & 7th St SW, Washington, DC 20560. This museum has a unique collection of modern and contemporary art and offers accessible tours and exhibits.

13:00 - Have lunch at Sweetgreen, located at 2221 I St NW, Washington, DC 20052. This restaurant offers healthy and customizable salads and bowls.

14:00 - Visit the Kennedy Center for the Performing Arts, located at 2700 F St NW, Washington, DC 20566. This accessible venue offers a variety of performances and cultural events, as well as tours of the facility.

16:00 - Take a walk around the Tidal Basin, located at 1501 Maine Ave SW, Washington, DC 20024. This accessible trail offers beautiful views of the Jefferson Memorial, the Washington Monument, and the cherry blossom trees in the spring.

18:00 - Have dinner at Founding Farmers, located at 1924 Pennsylvania Ave NW, Washington, DC 20006. This farm-to-table restaurant offers a variety of accessible dishes made with locally-sourced ingredients.

20:00 - Catch a movie at the AMC Georgetown, located at 3111 K St NW, Washington, DC 20007. This theater offers accessible seating and assistive listening devices for an enjoyable movie-going experience.

Day 3: Adaptive Outdoor Activities and Parks

8:00 AM - Start your day with breakfast at The Big Chair Cafe, located at 2122 Martin Luther King Jr Ave SE, Washington, DC 20020. This cafe offers a variety of breakfast options and is wheelchair accessible.

9:00 AM - Visit the United States Botanic Garden, located at 100 Maryland Ave SW, Washington, DC 20001. This garden offers a variety of plant collections and exhibits, and it is fully accessible.

11:00 AM - Head to the National Mall and visit the accessible monuments and memorials, including the Lincoln Memorial, Vietnam Veterans Memorial, and the Franklin Delano Roosevelt Memorial.

1:00 PM - Have lunch at the Mitsitam Cafe at the National Museum of the American Indian, located at 4th St & Independence Ave SW, Washington, DC 20560. This cafe offers a variety of Native American-inspired dishes and is wheelchair accessible.

2:00 PM - Visit the National Museum of African American History and Culture, located at 1400 Constitution Ave NW, Washington, DC 20560. This museum is fully accessible and has exhibits and artifacts related to African American history and culture.

4:00 PM - Take a walk around the Tidal Basin and see the accessible cherry blossom trees during peak bloom.

6:00 PM - Have dinner at Busboys and Poets, located at 2021 14th St NW, Washington, DC 20009. This restaurant offers a diverse menu with vegetarian and vegan options and is wheelchair accessible.

8:00 PM - Catch a show at the Kennedy Center, located at 2700 F St NW, Washington, DC 20566. This performing arts center offers accessible seating and services for guests with disabilities.

10:00 PM - Head back to your hotel for some rest and relaxation.

Day 4: Accessible Shopping and Dining Options

8:00 AM - Start your day with breakfast at Rise Bakery, located at 2409 18th St NW, Washington, DC 20009. This bakery offers a variety of gluten-free and vegan options.

9:00 AM - Head to CityCenterDC, located at 825 10th St NW, Washington, DC 20001. This open-air shopping center offers a variety of shops, including many with wheelchair accessibility and accessible restrooms.

11:00 AM - Take a short taxi ride to Union Market, located at 1309 5th St NE, Washington, DC 20002. This marketplace offers a variety of local vendors and restaurants, including many with accessible entrances and seating areas.

1:00 PM - Have lunch at Daikaya Ramen, located at 705 6th St NW, Washington, DC 20001. This restaurant offers a variety of Japanese cuisine, including gluten-free and vegetarian options.

2:00 PM - Head to the National Gallery of Art Sculpture Garden, located at Constitution Ave NW & 7th St NW, Washington, DC 20565. This outdoor sculpture garden is wheelchair accessible and offers a peaceful retreat from the city.

4:00 PM - Take a taxi to The Kennedy Center for the Performing Arts, located at 2700 F St NW, Washington, DC 20566. This performing arts center offers accessible seating and services for people with disabilities, and a variety of shows and performances.

7:00 PM - Have dinner at Marcel's, located at 2401 Pennsylvania Ave NW, Washington, DC 20037. This fine dining restaurant offers French cuisine and accessible seating options.

9:00 PM - End your evening with a drink at POV Rooftop Lounge and Terrace, located at 515 15th St NW, Washington, DC 20004. This rooftop bar offers beautiful views of the city and accessible seating options.

Thank You!

Thank you for joining us on this journey through Washington, D.C. We hope that this travel guide has provided you with valuable information and inspiration for planning your visit to the nation's capital. Whether you're interested in exploring the city's rich history, indulging in culinary delights, or immersing yourself in nature, D.C. has something for everyone. With a diverse array of cultural experiences and accessible attractions, it's a city that truly offers endless possibilities for exploration and enjoyment. We wish you a wonderful trip and unforgettable memories in Washington, D.C.!

Your friends at Guidora.

Copyright Notice

Guidora Washington DC in 3 Days Travel Guide ©

Disclaimer

The publishers have checked the information in this travel guide, but its accuracy is not warranted or guaranteed. Washington DC visitors are advised that opening times should always be checked before making a journey.

Tracing Copyright Owners

Every effort has been made to trace the copyright holders of referred material. Where these efforts have not been successful, copyright owners are invited to contact the Editor (Guidora) so that their copyright can be acknowledged and/or the material removed from the publication.

Creative Commons Content

We are most grateful to publishers of Creative Commons material, including images. Our policies concerning this material are (1) to credit the copyright owner, and provide a link where possible (2) to remove Creative Commons material, at once, if the copyright owner so requests - for example, if the owner changes the licensing of an image.

We will also keep our interpretation of the Creative Commons Non-Commercial license under review. Along with, we believe, most web publishers, our current view is that acceptance of the 'Non-Commercial' condition means (1) we must not sell the image or any publication containing the image (2) we may, however, use an image as an illustration for some information which is not being sold or offered for sale.

Note to other copyright owners

We are grateful to those copyright owners who have given permission for their material to be used. Some of the material comes from secondary and tertiary sources. In every case, we have tried to locate the original author or photographer and make the appropriate acknowledgment. In some cases, the sources have proved obscure and we have been unable to track them down. In these cases, we would like to hear from the copyright owners and will be pleased to acknowledge them in future editions or remove the material.

Printed in Great Britain
by Amazon

20612734R00088